DATE DUE

GAYLORD			PRINTED IN U.S.A.

THE ADDLED
PARLIAMENT OF
1614

Oxford University Press, Amen House, London E.C.4

GLASGOW NEW YORK TORONTO MELBOURNE WELLINGTON
BOMBAY CALCUTTA MADRAS KARACHI KUALA LUMPUR
CAPE TOWN IBADAN NAIROBI ACCRA

THE ADDLED PARLIAMENT OF 1614

BY

THOMAS L. MOIR

OXFORD
AT THE CLARENDON PRESS
1958

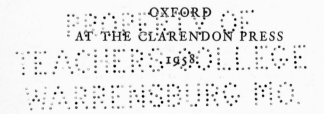

PRINTED IN GREAT BRITAIN
AT THE UNIVERSITY PRESS, OXFORD
BY CHARLES BATEY, PRINTER TO THE UNIVERSITY

TO

BERTA KATHERINE

Preface

THE origin of my interest in the Addled Parliament goes back to undergraduate and graduate work at the University of Minnesota under the direction of Professor David H. Willson. My interest in this parliament was stimulated by the preparation of a thesis entitled *The Members of Parliament from the Counties of Essex, Cambridge, and Huntingdon from 1604 to 1629*, which was submitted at the University of Minnesota in 1941 for the degree of M.A.

Although the Addled Parliament poses some fascinating problems, it has been almost neglected by recent historians. The only substantial account is one of about twenty-five pages written by S. R. Gardiner three-quarters of a century ago. D. H. Willson in *The Privy Councillors in the House of Commons 1604–1629* is interested in its preliminaries, but not in the parliament itself.

Dates in this work are given in old style except when the original document is dated in new style, but the year is always regarded as beginning on 1 January. In the case of documents dated in new style, both days of the month are given. Thus, a document dated 10 January 1613 old style in the original would appear as 10 January 1614. A document of the same date new style would appear 20 January 1614 in the original, but 10/20 January 1614 here.

The author's thanks are due to those who so patiently endured his many requests for obscure volumes, particularly to the staffs of the Trinity College, Dublin, library, the Institute of Historical Research, the British Museum, the Public Record Office, and the House of Lords. He is grateful to Mr. J. P. Cooper of Trinity College, Oxford, for transcripts of materials from the Wentworth Woodhouse papers. He is also indebted to Professor D. H. Willson for first interesting him in the field and for continued interest in his progress. Professor Willson has also read the first chapter and has made valuable suggestions for its revision. Finally, his gratitude is due to Professor T. W. Moody of Trinity College, Dublin, for patient and indispensable guidance.

T. L. M.

March 1957

Contents

I. THE CONSTITUTIONAL CRISIS   1

II. THE AGONIES OF DECISION   10

III. THE ELECTIONS   30

IV. THE NEW HOUSE OF COMMONS   55

V. THE HOUSE OF LORDS   62

VI. THE ROYAL PROGRAMME   67

VII. THE OPENING OF PARLIAMENT   78

VIII. UNDERTAKERS AND IMPOSITIONS   97

IX. *NOLI ME TANGERE*   114

X. THE EARL OF NORTHAMPTON AS IT WERE IN TRIUMPH   134

XI. THE ADDLED PARLIAMENT AND ROYAL POLICY   150

XII. THE ADDLED PARLIAMENT AND THE OPPOSITION   159

XIII. NEITHER AN END NOR A BEGINNING   163

NOTE ON BIBLIOGRAPHY   170

APPENDIX I. The Privy Council in 1614   174

APPENDIX II. The House of Lords in 1614   175

APPENDIX III. Corrections in the List of Members of the House of Commons in 1614   184

APPENDIX IV. The Official Group in the House of Commons   187

APPENDIX V. Connexions of the Peerage in the House of Commons   195

CONTENTS

APPENDIX VI. Abbreviated Genealogy of the
Howard Family   198

APPENDIX VII. Lists of Bills drawn up by the
Privy Council   200

INDEX   205

Chapter I

The Constitutional Crisis

THE Addled Parliament, the second parliament of James I, which lasted from 5 April to 7 June 1614, formed one of the links in the long chain of events stretching from 1603 to 1649. But the causes of the Civil War had roots striking much deeper than 1603, and the climax of 1649 was but one scene in a drama even then far from its conclusion.

For well over a century prior to 1603 the Tudor monarchs had governed England with conspicuous success. The Tudors had combined a strong monarchy with the machinery of parliament in a unique way. While they maintained their royal authority with the staunch support of public opinion, they allowed parliament to share in its exercise.

In this connexion it is well to bear in mind the significance of such concepts as 'the people' in the Tudor and early Stuart periods. While much of the political jargon of the twentieth century appeared at least as early as 1614, twentieth-century meanings must not be read into these expressions. When a speaker referred to 'the people' or even to a rudimentary concept of the social contract, he quite evidently had no idea of democracy in mind. Society meant the elements that controlled it. The nobility, the gentry, the urban middle classes, and perhaps the yeomanry were its only articulate elements. The great bulk of the population in both town and country had no voice and probably little interest in the great movements of the age.

A similar error must be avoided in our concepts of political life during this period. Because of linguistic limitations, terms such as 'party' and 'opposition leaders' are convenient to use. But nothing like the machinery of modern party politics must be read into them. A 'party' in 1614 was a loose and fluctuating group of individuals in general agreement on the major issues of the time. Its leaders were those who could best voice the sentiments of their fellows, or could usually exercise a personal dominance over them. But no organized body with set policies presented itself to the electors. The House of Commons was a group of individuals who often came to Westminster without clear opinions on many matters of public policy. The members of parliament represented the rising gentry, prosperous merchants, lawyers, and new officialdom of England in the sense that they were a typical cross-section of these elements.

The Tudors were able to dominate the government for a number of reasons. In the first place, the sixteenth century was a time of revolutionary change, particularly in religion, but also in economic organization and international relations. Internal upheavals in foreign lands were everywhere apparent to Tudor Englishmen, reviving memories of the Wars of the Roses. But England remained almost wholly free from these calamities, and its people believed that the Tudor monarchy had been their salvation.

In the second place, Tudor policies usually had popular support. The Tudor monarchy ruled essentially in the interests of the merchants and gentry. Henry VII crushed the nobility, and Henry VIII subjugated the Church, leaving the Tudors and their supporters triumphant.

The Tudors, then, fulfilled the aspirations of the merchants and gentry with a success so great that minor inconveniences were overlooked. While men might dislike Henry VII's extortionate financial methods or feel that Elizabeth's church settlement was too rigid, they believed that their position was the envy of all Europe. Although the weight of authority might gall, it did not crush them, and there could be no civil war with a strong hand at the helm. It was everywhere apparent that gentry, merchants, and officials were bound to the dynasty by common interests. Except during Mary's reign an essential harmony prevailed in England between governors and governed.

But the ability of the Tudors contributed much to this basic harmony. They had a genius for ruling: a combination of strength, tact, and showmanship, coupled with a keen understanding of human nature. Sensitive to public opinion, they were able to give concrete expression to the desires of their supporters. The support of these elements was all the more essential because local government was controlled by an unpaid group of non-professional officials drawn predominantly from the gentry. Governmental policies could become realities only with the support of the gentry.

The paradox in the strong Tudor monarchy was the development of parliament, the members of which came primarily from the gentry, the local governing class. By using parliament to effect their great reforms, the Tudors increased its stature in the eyes of the nation. Nevertheless they also devised machinery to control and direct parliamentary activities. Sessions of parliament were short, and with few exceptions no single parliament had a long existence. Thus frequent changes in membership checked the growth of corporate feeling. The Tudors did not lack men able and willing to support royal policy in the House of Commons. With an organized programme of legislation to present, these leaders succeeded in dominating the business of the House.

Elizabeth was adept at avoiding issues of principle. Unlike James I she was content to exercise the realities of power without concerning herself with constitutional theory. She was always willing to accept a compromise which saved the face of the House of Commons provided she gained her point, however indirectly. With tact and devious manœuvring Elizabeth kept latent opposition in check.

With the changing times after 1588, however, parliament became increasingly aware of its growing importance. But criticism of the government was held in abeyance partly through veneration for the Queen and partly through fear of the day when she would rule no more. The succession was far from clear, and memories of the past gave gloomy precedents for the future.

But when that day came, James of Scotland succeeded to the English throne with an ease which surprised many and pleased all. Anticipating a new golden age under a new dynasty, men failed to consider the problems of adjustment which faced King and country. Not the least of these problems was the man James Stuart. When it is realized that James was neither a pedant nor a fool, his character becomes the more difficult to understand. Although since childhood James had hoped to succeed his cousin on the throne of England, he had made little attempt to familiarize himself with English institutions. He was ignorant of the King's position in the English government, and he never acquired a fundamental under-

standing of the English political system. He never understood that the royal authority both in parliament and on
the local level rested on the voluntary co-operation of the
gentry class.

James had ruled with considerable success in Scotland.
When he reached manhood, he found himself a prince-
ling in a feudal state to which had been added a Presby-
terian kirk filled with all the unbending zeal of orthodox
Calvinism. But by adroit manipulation and deft intrigue
he was able to play faction against faction and gain the
support of moderate elements alarmed at the violence of
the kirk and some of the nobles. In the end by persistent
activities he made himself supreme over both kirk and
nobility. Yet in England, where he faced a far less desperate situation, he failed to find a solution.

James's failure in England came partly from his own
character and partly from the circumstances of the time.
His youthful experiences with Scottish Presbyterianism
had given him an exaggerated dislike and suspicion of
Protestant extremists and had blinded him to the difference between the violence of the Scots and the greater
moderation of the Puritans in England. He saw no more
reason than Elizabeth had seen for a larger comprehen-
sion in the Established Church.

James had developed his doctrine of the divine right of
kings to parry the claims of the Scottish kirk. This theory,
however, was ill adapted for dealing with the English
parliament. The King answered parliament's demands
with a blind and dogmatic conservatism, often rendered
more irritating by his superfluous excursions into constitutional theory. When he tried to govern England by the
methods successful in Scotland, he merely created a stale-
mate. Although James took a great interest in parliamen-

tary affairs, his undignified and tactless meddling irritated the House of Commons instead of guiding it.

Another defect in the new King's character was laziness. An abhorrence of governmental routine kept him from giving the administration the close day-to-day scrutiny that it demanded. Petulant and irritable, he had difficulty in following a consistent policy and was confused by conflicting advice, relying too much on favourites who pandered to his self-esteem. James was so harassed by suitors that whenever possible he fled to the country, leaving the government without a leader or a policy. Although the King faced many serious problems, the worst of them was his own character.

The changed international situation also had an impact on the relationship between King and parliament. By the time that James ascended the English throne, it became abundantly clear that the danger of foreign invasion was past. Although the issue had really been decided in 1588, the treaty with Spain in 1604 was the recognition of England's triumph. At the same time the conquest of Ireland secured one flank, while the Dutch republic protected the other. And with James's accession to the English throne, the ancient enemy to the north became a partner instead of a rival. By 1603 the foreign situation had ceased to be the major problem in English political life. Englishmen could now turn their attention to internal problems without endangering national security. Domestic abuses, neglected in time of peril, were everywhere ripe for reform.

Of the many problems before the King the religious question had the widest ramifications. In the early seventeenth century Englishmen had a panic fear of Popery, making them suspicious of alliances with Roman Catholic

6

powers and fearful of Roman Catholic influence at Court. The King's attitude towards the Puritans gave no comfort to those who feared the power of Rome. The bishops, realizing the dependence of the Establishment on royal protection, placed the full weight of ecclesiastical authority on the side of divine right.

The King also clashed with the House of Commons over privileges. Here James was forever raising fundamental constitutional questions. His doctrine of divine right, which he expounded on these occasions, seemed to the Commons to be a threat to the ancient constitution of England. Forced to justify themselves, they twisted and tortured medieval precedents to support their theories of parliamentary powers. This conflict, once aroused, necessarily went beyond privileges to the deeper questions of the relationship of Crown to Commons and of both to the state.

Another important sphere of conflict was public finance. Gifts to favourites and profiteering by tradesmen kept the royal treasury constantly on the verge of bankruptcy. But even under the parsimonious Elizabeth the ordinary revenue was inadequate, while rising prices and diminishing tax yields aggravated the problem. Elizabeth had been forced to sell Crown lands to meet war-time expenses, thus decreasing the resources inherited by her successor. In asking for larger grants of money the Crown had a better cause than it realized, but the Commons had not yet learned that good government has a price. They saw nothing but royal extravagances, and still fondly imagined that except in emergencies the King could live of his own.

The first parliament of James's reign was his longest, its five sessions stretching from 1604 to 1610. Little was done to elect royal supporters to this parliament, with the result that the official group was unusually weak. In particular, Sir Robert Cecil, the principal secretary of state, who had been the Crown's spokesman in the lower House during the latter part of Elizabeth's reign, had been elevated to the peerage in 1603. For a time early in 1606 only one privy councillor, the ineffectual 'Mr. Secondary' Herbert, was a member of the House of Commons, and the number of privy councillors never rose above two until 1610.

The only harmonious session of this parliament was that of 1605–6, held in the shadow of the Gunpowder Plot. In the other four sessions there were quarrels between King and Commons over elections, privileges, religion, monopolies, and impositions, coupled with grudging grants of money, while even such a statesmanlike proposal as the Scottish union failed of adoption.

The last two sessions of this parliament, both in 1610, were concerned primarily with the impositions question and the Great Contract. In 1606 the judges had decided that import duties or impositions levied on the authority of the Crown alone were legal, thus providing an extra-parliamentary source of revenue for the treasury. When parliament met in 1610, an attempt was made to settle the Crown's financial difficulties by the Great Contract. The King was to abandon most of his revenues from feudal tenures in return for a substantial revenue from parliament. But the Commons demanded that in addition impositions should be abolished. Although James offered to forgo any new impositions, he refused to give up those already in force. After offers and counter-offers, both sides lost patience, and the Great Contract broke down. This parliament finally came to an end late in 1610 amid feelings of frustration and bitterness on both sides. The King would need to exhibit tact and a spirit of compromise if the next parliament was to meet under conditions favourable to its success.

Chapter II

The Agonies of Decision

THE parliament of 1604, which had been adjourned on 24 November 1610, was finally dissolved on 9 February 1611. The only parliament to meet during the next decade was the Addled Parliament, which was summoned after delay, intrigue, and indecision on 16 February 1614. Nevertheless the ink was scarcely dry on the proclamation dissolving the previous parliament in 1611 before a new parliament was under consideration. As early as 11/21 January 1611 the Venetian ambassador reported plans for a new session. Again and again during the next three years rumours of a parliament passed from one courtier to another without a decision being made.

Meanwhile the government was making desperate attempts to keep the royal treasury solvent. Loans were sought, and it was hoped that the creation of baronets for a price would bring in enough revenue to make a parliament unnecessary. In August of 1612 Sir Thomas Parry, the chancellor of the Duchy, was placed at the head of a commission to devise projects for raising money. The commission considered debasing the coinage, the sale of Crown lands, compounding for wardships, and other schemes; but they searched in vain for a practical solution to the financial problem. In the end they had to admit that they could add only £35,776 to the ordinary revenue plus £309,681 from extraordinary sources. These sums would do little to reduce the debt of £500,000 and the annual deficit of £160,000. In spite of all that the commission could do, the treasury remained empty. It was this grinding pressure of financial necessity that finally forced James to summon the Addled Parliament.

From the first, proposals for a new parliament included plans to secure a more co-operative House of Commons than the previous one. On 11/21 January 1611 the Venetian ambassador wrote that measures would be taken to exclude those hostile to the King and obtain a pliable majority.

About this time Sir Henry Neville became a leading advocate of these proposals. Neville, a Berkshire gentleman, had served in six parliaments since 1584, including the parliament of 1604–11. He had also been ambassador to France 1599–1600. As a follower of the Earl of Essex and a friend of Prince Henry, he had reason to expect James's favour. Although Neville had not taken a prominent part in the parliament of 1604, his sympathies had been clearly with the opposition. In 1610 he had urged the King to accept the opposition's demands in regard to impositions and the Great Contract. But despite his friendship with many prominent opposition leaders in parliament, he was also on good terms with such courtiers as the brilliant Earl of Southampton, Lord Rochester, the King's favourite (Robert Carr, later the Earl of Somerset), and the ill-starred Sir Thomas Overbury.

John More in London, writing on 29 October 1611 to Sir Ralph Winwood, the English agent at The Hague, mentioned Neville's proposals for a parliament. More reported a rumour that Neville would be made secretary of state or at least a privy councillor through the influence of Overbury and Rochester. But he doubted the report partly because of Neville's 'unwieldy body and giving himself to a mere country life'. A more important obstacle to Neville's advancement was his activity in parliament in 1610.

> . . . He did not . . . speak in Parliament for the King's demands, but ranged himself with those Patriots that were accounted of a contrary faction to the Courtiers; which I think he would not have done, if he had aspired to any Court employment.... The plot was ... that Sir H. Neville should undertake to deal with the Lower House, and then (so as my Lord Treasurer would not intermeddle) there was no doubt but that better effects would come of the next Session (which is like to be in February next) than did come of the former....[1]

All the elements of Neville's parliamentary programme appeared in this letter in their strength and weakness except his detailed plans for conciliating the lower House. Even the word 'undertake' occurs here for the first time in connexion with the Addled Parliament. But Neville faced serious problems in carrying out his programme. He was unpopular at Court both as one who did not 'belong' and as an opposition figure in parliament in 1610. His dependence on Overbury and Rochester bred jealousy, and he was at odds with Salisbury. Finally, his activity was limited by the crippling physical weaknesses that Chamberlain noted in 1614. Although Neville's parliamentary programme may have been basically sound, even in 1611 he faced well-nigh insuperable obstacles to its realization.[2]

By the summer of 1612 Neville had given his programme so definite a form that he was in a position to approach the King directly. He had one conference with James in July and a second in September. Advised by his

---

[1] *H.M.C. Buccleuch MSS.* i. 102 (Winwood papers).
[2] *Letters of Chamberlain,* i. 509–10.

friends to proceed cautiously, the second time he took care to see the King on the hunting field, where he might expect to find James in a favourable mood.

> ... Sir H. [N]evill had speech [with his] Majesty as he hunted, for two hours, and received good approbation in the most of his advices, and by conference made good the rest. ...

Meanwhile Neville also conferred with the leaders of the parliamentary opposition of 1610, including Sir Maurice Berkeley and Sir Robert Phelips, in the hope of gaining their support for his proposals.[3]

The proposals which Neville presented to the King had two sections: the first was intended to convince James that a parliament should be summoned; the second was a list of specific concessions. In the first section Neville began by analysing the breach with parliament in 1610. He pointed out that James's prestige had suffered both at home and abroad:

> ... I consider in what termes the king and the last Parliament parted at the dissolution: full of distast & Acrimony on his Majestys part, and not without some discontentment on theirs. I consider also, that from the Parliament the Apprehensions, that are taken there, are spread & dispersed over the whole Realm. And further, that the knowledg of these misunderstandings between his Majesty, and the Parliament is not confined within this kingdome only, but is flown abroad into all forreign parts, that have any commerce, or dealing with us. Now What disadvantage this opinion may breed us, and what hopes it is like to raise both in our Enemies abroad, and our discontented Persons at home, may easily bee gathered

---

[3] *H.M.C. Buccleuch MSS.* i. 112–14 (Winwood papers); *Commons jn.* i. 485; Phelips MSS. quoted in Farnham, 'Somerset Election of 1614', in *E.H.R.* xlvi. 581 n. (Oct. 1931).

for as there is nothing that more upholds the reputation of any Prince than the opinion of his strength at home, which consisteth principally in the Love & concord between him and his People from whence there followeth naturally a sequence of all other duties on their part, to make him strong and able to help or hurt his neighbours. So there is nothing that emboldeneth more an Enemy either open, or secret to attempt the disturbance of the Peace of any State, than the Imagination, that the Prince and People stand not in kind and loving termes together. . . .[4]

Consequently Neville maintained that only through a harmonious session of parliament could the breach be repaired. While Neville recognized that a new parliament might again prove intractable, he felt that he was well enough acquainted with many of its leaders to know that they were not so opposed to the royal policies as they seemed.

. . . So as I dare undertake for the most of them, that the kings Majestys proceeding in a gratious course toward his People, shall finde those gentlemen exceeding willing to doe him service & to give him such contentment as may sweeten all the former Distasts, & leave both his Majesty & the World fully satisfied of their own good Intentions, & of the generall affection of his Subjects It is true (as I lately delivered unto his Majesty) that some things will bee desired & expected of him by way of Grace which may both give some contentment to them that shall pay what is given, & justify the care, & honest regard of them, that shall give it. And without this I dare promise nothing. . . .

Neville had drawn up a list of concessions after consultation with leaders of the opposition. He believed that

___

[4] P.R.O. S.P.D. 14/74: 44. See also Carte, *History of England*, iv. 17 and n.

these concessions, which he presented to the King in an accompanying memorial, would be welcomed by the people without costing the Crown anything of fundamental importance. He also felt that with careful management the supply question could be settled in the first four or five weeks of the session. Neville recommended that the King should be careful not to irritate parliament in his speeches and should act as if he were sure of their goodwill and affection. Grievances complained of in the last parliament should be reformed, and the King should be careful to carry out all promises made in 1610. The King should deal directly with the House of Commons or through its own members instead of approaching it through the Lords. Also the Commons should be allowed to name the members of committees which conferred with the King, and the action of a committee should not bind the House.

Apart from the list of concessions, these were the main points in Neville's programme, which formed the basis of fact behind the rumours of undertaking in the Addled Parliament. In the light of subsequent charges in the House of Commons, one thing is striking: there was no suggestion of a plan to influence elections or pack the House of Commons. In fact Neville's programme was based on the opposite idea of conciliating the leaders of the opposition of 1610. He spoke of 'the principall & most understanding Gentlemen, that were of the last Parliament and are like to bee of this'. Thus he anticipated that the leaders in 1610 would be chosen once more. He based his hopes of success on his friendship with them and on their support of his programme.

The memorial which accompanied these proposals contained a list of concessions plus eight items which the

King had offered to parliament in November of 1610. These concessions would reform minor grievances in the operation of the government without attacking fundamental problems. The significant ones would protect the holders of land from suits brought by the Crown over technical defects in their titles, and would give individuals protection against extortionate royal officials. The most important point concerned impositions. Neville proposed that this controversy should be settled by an agreement not to increase impositions without the consent of parliament.[5]

But even such a modest programme went too far for the King, who merely procrastinated. In 1613 Neville made a new attempt to win James's support. This time he proposed a similar series of minor administrative reforms to be granted before parliament met as a conciliatory gesture. He also drew up another copy of the concessions to the House of Commons which he had suggested earlier, omitting only his suggestion for settling the imposition question. Neville also begged the help of Rochester (Robert Carr) in persuading the King to accept his programme. Neville pointed out rather uncharitably that the Earl of Salisbury, who had died in May of 1612, could be blamed for all of James's unpopular actions. He also advised against any new projects for raising money because they produced more irritation than cash. But Neville suggested that such royal rights as wardship should be vigorously enforced, so that the King could obtain more from the Commons if he agreed to give them up. He also sent a memorial to the King defending his suggested compromise on the imposition question by pointing out that the King would take the initiative in

[5] P.R.O. S.P.D. 14/74:46.

the settlement, and that present revenues would be left untouched.[6]

This, then, was the programme by which Neville hoped to gain the co-operation of the Commons. Its defects were immediately obvious. Again and again Neville reiterated that the King would give up nothing of importance. He had to devise a list of concessions which would be acceptable to the King because they cost him nothing, and which would still induce the Commons to grant James his needed revenue. Neville was faced with the insoluble problem of reconciling the irreconcilable.

What is apparent at once from these proposals is their failure to grapple with the real issues at stake between Crown and Commons. Neville made no attempt to deal with such questions as Church reform, monopolies, or purveyance. Nor was there any suggestion of satisfying the Commons on the question of recusants. Neville's tentative solution for the imposition question embroiled him with the King even though it probably would not have satisfied the opposition. All of the proposed concessions would have removed small irritations and would have reformed minor abuses, but Neville can hardly have regarded them as a real basis for settlement. Probably he felt that he must persuade the King to summon parliament as the first step towards a solution. Without a parliament there was no hope of improvement. But once parliament met, he might be able to win over both sides to a compromise solution. Any programme, however hopeless in itself, would serve Neville's purpose if he could use it to persuade the King to summon parliament.

The other great proponent of a parliament during these

[6] B.M. Cott. MSS. Titus F iv, ff. 344, 346, 349, 350.

17

years was Sir Francis Bacon, still only a comparatively minor official. Bacon approached the King only a week after the death, on 24 May 1612, of the Earl of Salisbury, James's chief minister. He suggested that the King should summon a parliament, and made a bid to become James's parliamentary manager.

> ... Now because I take myself to have a little skill in that region [i.e. in parliament], as one that ever affected that your Majesty mought in all your causes not only prevail, but prevail with satisfaction of the inner man; and though no man can say but I was a perfect and peremptory royalist, yet every man makes me believe that I was never one hour out of credit with the lower house: my desire is to know, whether your Majesty will give me leave to meditate and propound unto you some preparative remembrances touching the future Parliament. ...[7]

This bid failed, but the next year Bacon tried again. He drew up a private memorandum on parliament, and then presented a revised version of it to the King. The revised version had two sections: the first section contained reasons for summoning a parliament, and the second included suggestions for controlling it. In the first section Bacon declared that old grievances had become dead issues, and few new ones had appeared.

> ... I do not find since the last Parliament any new action of estate amongst your Majesty's proceedings that hath been harsh or distasteful: and therefore seeing the old grievances (having been long broached) cannot but wax dead and flat, and that there hath been no new matter either to rub up and revive the old or to give other cause of discontent, I think the case much amended to your Majesty's advantage. ...[8]

[7] Spedding, *Letters and Life of Bacon*, iv. 279–80.
[8] Ibid. 369–70.

Bacon also believed that the opposition of 1610 had gone to pieces. But of those he mentioned as converts to the royal cause, Lawrence Hyde, Sir Dudley Digges, and Sir John Holles all joined the opposition in the Addled Parliament, while Sir Edwin Sandys was more clearly the opposition leader in 1614 than he had been in 1610. Furthermore Christopher Brooke, whom Bacon declared to be dead, proved to be remarkably lively in the 1614 session. Bacon sadly over-estimated the disintegration of the opposition. He also maintained that the Great Contract of 1610 had strained relations with parliament because of its bargaining spirit. Bacon concluded this section with an unwarranted charge that the Earl of Salisbury had deliberately stirred up parliamentary opposition for his own ends:

... Lastly, I cannot excuse him that is gone [Salisbury] of an artificial animating of the Negative; which infusion or influence now ceasing I have better hope. ...

Bacon reiterated his belief that the King should not haggle like a merchant. He urged that in any case James should end the session in harmony because he could cultivate the goodwill of the Commons only little by little. Bacon's next suggestion was that the session should be 'a little reduced to the more ancient form'. By this somewhat enigmatic phrase he meant that the ostensible reason for summoning parliament should not be the King's financial needs. The House of Commons should be given other problems to debate, such as the stimulation of commerce or the plantation of Ireland. The King should also declare that he had other financial resources than parliamentary grants to reduce his dependence on

the House of Commons. Finally, Bacon condemned electioneering practices:

... Also that there be no brigues [solicitation by underhand methods] nor canvasses, whereof I hear too much;
for certainly howsoever men may seek to value their service
in that kind, it will but increase animosities and oppositions;
and besides will make whatsoever shall be done to be in evil
conceit amongst your people in general afterwards. ...

Bacon was not entirely candid with the King. His
private memorandum on parliament drawn up about the
same time was similar to the memorandum to the King,
but it contained in addition a series of twenty-one 'Incidents of a Parliament' which he did not reveal to James.
These suggestions give further clues to Bacon's plans for
managing the House of Commons.

Despite his condemnation of electoral manipulation in
the royal memorandum, Bacon proposed to influence the
choice of members of parliament. His private memorandum included these suggestions:

12. What persons in particular, in respect of their gravity,
discretion, temper, and ability to persuade, are fit to
be brought in to be of the house, *bonis artibus*, without
labouring or packing.
What persons in particular, as violent and turbulent,
are fit to be kept back from being of the house, *bonis
artibus*, without labouring or packing.
13. What use may be made of the Boroughs of the Cinq
Ports, and of the Duchy, and other boroughs at the
devotion of diverse the K's counsellors, for the
placing persons well affected and discreet.
14. What use may be made of the unlawful custom and
abuse, for the sending up and returning of blanques

[i.e. the practice by which a borough would send its election writ blank to some influential man and allow him to insert the name of his nominee], which if it be restrained perchance it may stumble many a one's entrance that think themselves assured of places.

[15.] What course may be taken that though the K. do use such providence as is before remembered and leave not things to chance, yet it may be so handled as it may have no shew nor scandal nor nature of the packing or briguing [soliciting by underhand means] of a Parliament truly free and not packed against him.[9]

This memorandum also suggested that something should be done to win over, or at least silence, various elements in the House of Commons. Bacon mentioned specifically lawyers, merchants, justices of the peace, and country gentlemen. He also considered how the 'popular party' of 1610 could be weakened or dissolved, and how he could prevent the formation of party factions. Aware of the weaknesses of the official *bloc* in the parliament of 1604, he suggested more privy councillors in the House of Commons, an experienced Speaker, and also

What course may be taken for the drawing of that body of the house which consisteth of courtiers and the K's servants to be as they have ever been in former times (except the last Parliament) used to be, that is, sure and zealous for the K. and not (as they were then) fearful or popular. . . .

As to the imposition question, which Bacon had referred to only parenthetically in his memorandum to the King, here he simply said, 'The Impositions and how that

___
[9] Spedding, *Letters and Life of Bacon*, iv. 366-8.

matter may be buried and silenced', scarcely a solution to the problem.

Bacon's suggestions for influencing elections are particularly interesting because of the storm over undertakers in the Addled Parliament and the criticism there of the sort of practices that Bacon privately favoured. Also it is hard to see how the suggestions in Bacon's private memorandum differed from those election practices which he himself condemned after the failure of the Addled Parliament. Although the rumours of undertaking in 1614 grew out of Neville's proposals, Neville made no suggestions for manipulating elections. Bacon's proposals more nearly resembled the schemes that the Commons laid at the door of the undertakers.

Bacon's programme, like Neville's, was not without defects. The most serious of them was his lack of imagination where public opinion was concerned. Like many other great and wise men Bacon did not understand the mentality of his opponents, and of the articulate portion of society as a whole. He believed that the opposition in parliament was merely a faction which represented nothing fundamental in English society. Once its leaders had been wooed away and minor concessions had satisfied different sections of the Commons, the opposition would wither away like the rootless thing that it was.

Bacon also believed that Englishmen had short memories and could be influenced by such primitive propaganda methods as the Crown had at its disposal. According to him in three years the grievances of 1610 had lost their appeal because they had not been debated in parliament. Despite general knowledge of the King's penury, he believed he could convince men that the King was not forced to summon parliament because of lack of money.

Bacon faced another problem in dealing with the King. He had to persuade James to summon parliament without disclosing his real plans for managing it. The King would oppose any realistic programme, yet without the King's consent there would be no parliament at all. In the final analysis Bacon did not realize (or perhaps would not admit even to himself) that James was incapable of filling the kingly role assigned to him in the Baconian theory of government.

The King's hesitation in making the decision was reinforced during the years 1612–14 by a series of incidents which more than once were the ostensible reasons for delaying a parliament. The summons seemed imminent in the spring of 1612 when the Earl of Salisbury, both principal secretary and treasurer, fell ill and died on 24 May. Contention over the choice of a new secretary lasted until a few days before the Addled Parliament met, and was closely connected with the question of summoning it. Candidates for the secretaryship were numerous. They included such prominent figures as Bacon, Sir Charles Cornwallis, Sir Thomas Edmondes, Sir John Holles, Sir William Waad, and old Sir John Herbert, the ineffective second secretary.

But by the late summer of 1612 the serious candidates were reduced to four: Sir Henry Neville, Sir Ralph Winwood, Sir Henry Wotton, and Sir Thomas Lake. Winwood, a career diplomat, had been ambassador to France in 1601–2, and since 1603 had served as the English agent at The Hague. Wotton, a half-brother of Lord Wotton, who had been a privy councillor since 1602, was also a career diplomat. He had served as ambassador to Venice since 1604. Although he was to end his days in holy orders as provost of Eton, he is perhaps best remembered as an author and as Izaak Walton's companion at angling. Lake, a protégé of the influential Howard family, became a minor official in 1600. By 1612 he had risen to the post of keeper of the records at Whitehall.

The King was pulled this way and that by the various Court factions, and could not decide whom to choose as secretary. In the end he decided to put his 'kingcraft' into practice. As John Chamberlain wrote as early as 11 June 1612:

... the King in this distraction makes no haste to nominate any [as secretary] but says he is prettelie skilled in the craft himself, and till he be thoroughly wearie will execute yt in person....[10]

For almost two years James acted as his own secretary, relying on Rochester (Sir Robert Carr) for advice and on Lake for clerical assistance. The new secretary was not finally appointed until 29 March 1614, just a week before the Addled Parliament met.

The choice of Lake to assist the King was a partial victory for the Howard family and the pro-Spanish faction at Court. The Howards, a worthless and treacherous lot, vied with Rochester for dominance at Court. By 1614 they held six peerages and three places on the privy council. In addition Elizabeth Howard had been married to Lord Knollys, a privy councillor, since 1605. In 1613 the Howards were reconciled with Somerset (Rochester) when he married Frances Howard after her divorce from the Earl of Essex.[11]

The leading figure in the Howard family was Henry, the aged Earl of Northampton, already beyond his seventieth year. A born master of intrigue, Northampton

[10] *Letters of Chamberlain*, i. 355.
[11] For an abbreviated genealogy of the Howard family see Appendix VI.

secured a strong influence over the King through supple-
ness, flattery, and a stupendous lack of principle. Even
though his father and elder brother had both been executed for treason, James created him an earl in 1604.
Northampton was secretly a Roman Catholic, and was
in Spanish pay even while negotiating the peace treaty
with Spain in 1604. With the rest of his family he was
opposed to summoning parliament after 1610 because he
feared that it would strengthen anti-Spanish sentiment
and force the King into a war with Spain. Northampton
did his best to embroil King and parliament in 1614. He
lived just long enough to witness the success of his intrigues, dying only a week after the dissolution.

By promoting factional strife in the privy council the
Howards were able to further Spanish interests. They
eventually secured the support of Somerset, Lord Knollys, Lord Wotton, and the Earl of Worcester for the
Spanish interest. Lord Chancellor Ellesmere, Archbishop
Abbot, the Earl of Pembroke, and perhaps Lord Zouch
and Sir Julius Caesar formed the Protestant faction on the
council. The three Scots on the English privy council,
Lennox, Fenton, and Dunfermline, were partisans of
France. Split into factions and immersed in an atmosphere
both venal and mercenary, the council could not even
keep its own secrets. It busied itself with routine administrative duties while the King turned to favourites for
advice on matters of state.

The Spanish faction at Court took advantage of every
chance happening to delay a parliament. The death of
Salisbury and the delay in appointing a new secretary
postponed any chance of a session until the autumn of
1612. Then the death of Prince Henry on 17 November
1612 produced a new delay even though in the long run

it increased the pressure for a parliament. It ended the hope that the dowry of the Prince's bride might ease James's financial plight. So desperate had the King's financial predicament become that even his son's marriage was considered in terms of its cash value.[12] In 1613 the marriage of James's daughter Elizabeth to the Elector Palatine and the meeting of the Irish parliament provided new excuses for delay.

Meanwhile the Howards played on James's fears to postpone parliament. In the late summer of 1613 at a meeting of the privy council Northampton advised the King

. . . That he should in no case call together and ioyne his Enemies; for suche were those of ye Parlament, that would doe nothing which hee desired, as hee had seen by experience. And that hee knewe, That thei did already censure and mur-mure at his Actions, bothe for having solde ye Titles of Baronetts, and for having raysed those summs of Money, with muche attention. And afterward calling him aside, tolde him; Hee had spoaken with muche freenes, but with as muche truthe. . . .[13]

By this time also the Countess of Essex (Frances Howard) had persuaded Rochester as well to throw his influence on the side of the Spanish faction.

But by the end of 1613 the King's financial plight was desperate. Officials were unpaid, and day-to-day expenses had to be met by the sale of Crown lands while ingenious amateurs tried in vain to locate new sources of revenue. Chamberlain wrote to Sir Dudley Carleton on 9 Decem-ber 1613:

[12] *Letters of Chamberlain*, i. 391.
[13] P.R.O. S.P. Spanish 94/20 (Digby to King James 22 Sept. 1613, extracts from Sarmiento's dispatch of 6 Sept. 1613 from England).

... we are here in great straights for monie, so that your brother William with all his diligence ... cannot yet procure your allowance [as an ambassador] but is fooded on with fayre wordes and promises from weeke to weeke and day to day, till he is almost tired with the care and trouble. Neither can he tell where justly to lay the fault, but only on the present want and necessitie, which is such, that the very guard that attends the King's person now at Roiston, and the poore posts that trot up and downe, are far behind, and besides clamoring and murmuring, have made many fruitles petitions to the King himself for theyr pay. Neither is there any great hope of amendment, seeing that so many projects that have ben set on foote succeed not but for the most part come to nothing, and the devisers and projecters that promised mountaines do in the end *restar con tanto di naso*; only the surest way, and which hitherto fayles not is sale of lands, ... wherwith the Lords Commissioners for the treasurie meant to have stopt some gapps. ... [14]

In the face of such grinding necessity even Somerset[15] and the Spanish faction could stave off the inevitable no longer. By late January the issue seemed so certain that opposition leaders were gathering in London.

... There is a generall voyce and almost certain expectation of a parlement twixt this [20 January 1614] and Easter, and the great colonells of that militia muster themselves alredy, and begin to shew about the towne; but the certain and finall resolution of that busines is saide to be now in hand at Audley-end, whence the oracle must come twixt this and Sonday. ... [16]

But characteristically after two weeks of vacillation

---

[14] *Letters of Chamberlain*, i. 490.
[15] Viscount Rochester was created Earl of Somerset in November 1613.
[16] *Letters of Chamberlain*, i. 502.

James went off to the country, leaving the decision in the hands of the council.

The council itself spent almost two weeks in bringing the issue to a conclusion. By this time the Spanish faction, aware that it could delay a parliament no longer, threw its opponents off balance by an abrupt change of front. As Northampton wrote to Somerset, who was with the King:

> ... It was made cleer [in the council] to the stupifaction of somebody [Pembroke?] that no man ever doubted of the good that a parlament well affected ought to yealde. ... To be playne with your Lordship so many difficulties arise upon the contemplation of this subiecte as if thear wear possibility in repairinge or supporting the king's estate by any other means the greater parte of us wolde holde this time worse fitted and the meanes lesse prepared then we wold wish befor the parliamente wear agreed upon.
>
> But necessity which drawes men to please themselves with probabilities and to wave inconveniences will perhappes drawe us to adventur rather than to suffer. ... [17]

The council debated the whole question of parliament on three separate occasions during the second week in February. In the first day's debate reasons for and against a parliament were discussed. In general the council felt that the situation was no more favourable than it had been in 1610. Although no one was particularly hopeful of a successful parliament, all other means of raising revenue had been exhausted.

The council met for a second time on Saturday of the same week (12 February). At this meeting ways of managing parliament were considered, and the council took up the proposals of Neville and Bacon. A decision

[17] B.M. Cott. MSS. Titus F iv, ff. 329–30.

was finally reached the next day. No one objected to a parliament although some were doubtful of a favourable outcome. The date of 5 April was chosen for the opening of the session. As time was short, Northampton wrote to Somerset, who was with the King, asking for quick approval of the date so that a warrant to issue the writs could be prepared for James's signature.[18]

Somerset replied at once that the King preferred 10 April as the date for the opening of parliament. On Wednesday, 16 February, Northampton reassembled the council, which drew up an account of the whole debate, including reasons why 5 April was preferable to a later date. They felt that 10 April was too near Passion Week (17–23 April), and that all important matters in the English parliament should be settled before the Irish parliament met on 3 May. Considering the pressure of time, the council asked the King for an immediate decision. Probably the warrant for the issue of the writs accompanied this letter, for it had been returned to the council with the King's signature by Saturday. But he must have signed it in a fit of abstraction, as he complained a few days later that he did not know what the council had decided. The writs, none of which are known to exist, were issued on Monday, 21 February, although they were dated the previous Saturday.[19]

So at last, after three years of expedients, indecision, and intrigue, the die was cast. The King had decided to summon once more the only organ of the English government which reflected the temper of his subjects.

[18] Ibid., ff. 331–2; P.R.O. S.P.D. 14/76: 22.
[19] Ibid. 14/76: 24; P.R.O. St. Ch. 8/293: 11; B.M. Cott. MSS. Titus C vi, f. 107; Titus F iv, f. 342.

Chapter III

The Elections

ALTHOUGH the decision to summon parliament was not made until 16 February, ambitious candidates had already begun to canvass for seats. On 13 February the corporation of Rochester offered Somerset a seat there, and although the Earl of Northampton canvassed Totnes on the twentieth, he was already too late.

The elections themselves, the first in a decade, produced many contests and much bitterness. As early as 19 February unsettling rumours caused a panic at Court. Courtiers told the King that the gentry in the shires were using all their influence against candidates put forward by the Crown. The parliament would be so filled with hostile members that it would be better to postpone it. Even though James ordered members of the privy council to use their influence in his name, later reports stated that even in smaller boroughs letters from prominent persons were having less influence than expected.[1]

An analysis of the elections does not, however, bear out these rumours spread at Court. It is quite possible that the unsettling reports were spread by the Spanish faction in a final attempt to frighten the King into changing his mind about parliament.

Although a wider franchise made county elections less subject to official pressure than borough elections, the Crown gained many successes and suffered few setbacks in the shires. Three of the four privy councillors in the

[1] Nichols, *Progresses of King James*, ii. 755; *Letters of Chamberlain*, i. 517–19.

House of Commons sat for counties, and many other county members had connexions at Court. In Berkshire, for example, the Court faction secured both seats, one going to Sir Thomas Parry, a privy councillor, and the other to Sir Henry Neville, a leading candidate for the secretaryship. In Middlesex official pressure avoided a threatened contest. The two official candidates were Sir Julius Caesar, a privy councillor, and Sir Thomas Lake, who missed the secretaryship, but became a member of the council on 29 March. One opposition candidate, Sir Walter Cope, the master of the wards, withdrew from the contest. (Parry secured a seat at Stockbridge for him.) But pressure from the King was used to force Sir Francis Darcy out of the race. Caesar and Lake were chosen, but Darcy had his revenge in 1620 when he carried Middlesex against a privy councillor.

In Kent there was a spirited contest between Sir Thomas Walsingham, keeper of the Queen's wardrobe, and Sir Edwin Sandys, prominent in the 1610 opposition. By unanimous choice the first seat in the shire went to Sir Peter Manwood, more a scholar than a politician. Sandys had support from both sides. Sir Robert Mansell, treasurer of the navy, and Sir Dudley Digges, a prominent opposition leader, both used their influence on his behalf. But despite their combined efforts he failed to secure the seat and withdrew from the contest.

Although Puritanism was strong in Buckinghamshire and Essex, Court candidates were successful in both places. In Buckinghamshire Sir Francis Goodwin, whom the council had supported in a by-election of 1606, was chosen. In Essex the two knights were Sir Robert Rich and Sir Richard Weston, both with Court connexions. In Oxfordshire, where Roman Catholicism was strong, the two seats went to Sir John Croke, the son of a justice of the King's Bench, and to Sir Anthony Cope, a prominent Puritan. In Caernarvonshire Richard Wynn of a prominent local family was elected even though he was a follower of the Earl of Suffolk (Thomas Howard), the lord chamberlain.

Many other county seats were held by persons with Court connexions. Sir George More, the chancellor of the Order of the Garter and the most active royal supporter in this parliament, sat for Surrey, where the Earl of Nottingham (Charles Howard) had great influence as lord-lieutenant. Sir Thomas Howard, a relative of Nottingham and master of the Prince's horse, sat for Wiltshire. Sir Roger Wilbraham, a master of requests, was elected in Cheshire. Gloucestershire returned Sir William Cooke, a clerk of the liveries. Sir Thomas Jermyn, a courtier and perennial office-seeker, represented Puritan Suffolk. Another courtier representing a Puritan county was the eldest son of Lord Hunsdon, Sir Henry Carey, who sat for Hertfordshire. Sir Oliver Cromwell, the protector's royalist uncle, was elected as usual in Huntingdonshire. Two other courtiers, Sir William Cavendish, second son of Lord Cavendish, and Henry Howard, a son of the Earl of Suffolk, sat for Derbyshire. Cumberland elected Sir Thomas Penruddock, a courtier. Sir Thomas Gerrard, who became a gentleman of the Queen's privy chamber about 1615, was elected in Lancashire. Sir James Scudamore, captain of Kidwelly Castle in Wales, sat for Herefordshire. Sir William Selby, a member for Northumberland, was a royal pensioner. Carmarthenshire elected Sir Robert Mansell, treasurer of the navy.

But not all the county members with Court connexions supported royal policies in parliament. Sir John Holles of Nottinghamshire, who had been comptroller of Prince Henry's household, lost favour after the Prince's death and had joined the opposition by 1614. Sir Herbert Croft, who sat for Herefordshire, later declared vociferously that he had supported the Crown in 1614, but the records belie his protests.

In some few counties, however, Crown candidates met difficulties. The fiercest contest of all raged in Somerset, where Sir Edward Phelips, the master of the rolls, tried to force his son Sir Robert on his home county. Sir Edward, who represented the county in 1604–11 when he was Speaker, no doubt wished to secure his son's political inheritance. But Sir Maurice Berkeley, who represented the county in 1601, and John Poulett, who won a by-election there in 1610, considered that they had a better claim. Also, Poulett maintained just before the election that the county seemed well disposed towards him and Berkeley, and asked them to stand. While Berkeley and Poulett joined forces against young Phelips, Sir Edward used all his influence for his son and staked his reputation on the result. He rallied to his support most of the justices, the Earls of Hertford and Rutland, Lord Arundell, and James Montague, the Bishop of Bath and Wells. Nevertheless, despite attempts at trickery by Phelips and his associates, Berkeley and Poulett were successful.[2]

This story has an ironical sequel. Sir Robert Phelips, who fell back on a seat at Saltash, opposed the Court so violently in 1614 that he broke his father's heart, and in the 1620's he became one of the real leaders of the opposition. Berkeley, who had inclined toward the opposition in the previous parliament, took a moderate course in

---

[2] *Letters of Chamberlain*, i. 517–19, 521, 523–4; Farnham, 'Somerset Election 1614' in *E.H.R.* xlvi. 579–99 (Oct. 1931).

1614, but died three years later. Poulett, who took little part in the parliament of 1614, became a baron in 1627 and fought for King Charles in the Civil War. So in the long run the Court's defeat was more apparent than real.

A Court candidate was also defeated in Lincolnshire. Here Sir Thomas Monson, the keeper of the naval arsenal in the Tower, contested the county against Sir George Manners, a brother of the Earl of Rutland, and Sir Peregrine Bertie, a brother of Lord Willoughby de Eresby. Against such a powerful combination of local interests headed by his social superiors, Monson quite naturally failed despite his family connexions in Lincolnshire. But here again the Court's defeat was not significant because both Manners and Bertie had relationships and interests which would lead them to support the Crown.

Sir Henry Rich, a favourite of the King, was defeated in Norfolk. Rich entered the contest confidently, supported by letters from the lord chamberlain, Thomas Howard, Earl of Suffolk. The sheriff's county court opened at the castle in Norwich, the customary place, on 7 March at about seven o'clock in the morning with about three thousand freeholders assembled for the election, most of them supporters of Rich. But within half an hour, after some routine business had been dispatched, the sheriff's deputy suddenly adjourned the court to Swaffham, twenty miles away. The high sheriff, who was already at Swaffham, proceeded to hold the election there in the presence of a few freeholders assembled for the purpose. Before eight o'clock in the morning two young knights, Sir Henry Bedingfield and Sir Hamon L'Estrange, had been elected. This manœuvre, although a trick of the sheriff, was apparently legal, and Rich finally found a seat at Leicester borough.

Here again local interests triumphed over outside influence, for both L'Estrange and Bedingfield belonged to leading families of Norfolk gentry. But the election has interesting sidelights. Probably Sir Henry Rich had sufficient support to be elected. The 'popular' candidates succeeded only because they tricked the Court candidate. Also in a county with many Puritans, a near-recusant was chosen. Although Sir Henry Bedingfield was a conformist in 1614, he was a recusant most of his life. Even where Puritanism was strong, family prestige outweighed religious differences. Finally, both successful candidates came from strong royalist families, and both suffered for their loyalty during the Civil War.[3]

In Hampshire Sir Henry Wallop was defeated by Sir William Uvedale and Sir Richard Tichbourne. Wallop, a Hampshire squire, must have had connexions at Court, for Sir Thomas Parry secured a seat for him at Stockbridge when he failed in Hampshire. Uvedale was a favourite of Somerset and a minor officeholder. Tichbourne was a member of a prominent Hampshire family which included many recusants and enjoyed the favour of James I.

The real contest was between Wallop and Tichbourne. As soon as news of a new parliament reached the county, feverish electioneering began on both sides. Tichbourne secured two great advantages at the start: he persuaded Uvedale to join forces with him against Wallop; and he secured the aid of the sheriff, Sir Richard Norton, the steward of the Bishop of Winchester. On the other side Wallop circulated slanderous tales about

[3] *Letters of Chamberlain*, i. 517–19; *Commons jn.* i. 457; *Catholic Record Society Miscellany*, vi. 1–3, 431. See also the election petition for Norfolk calendared in *H.M.C. Rept. 4*, appendix, supplemental calendar.

Tichbourne, probably accusing him of Roman Catholicism.[4]

The election was held on 21 March in the hall of Winchester Castle, which was leased by the Tichbourne family. The Tichbourne faction adopted every available device to defeat Wallop. First they packed the hall with their own supporters. Then, after Wallop demanded a poll, they took a view of the electors, but instructed their followers to confuse the picture by walking back and forth from one group to the other. Finally and with great reluctance the sheriff agreed to a poll, but he detained the voters all day before taking it. Although food was given to the supporters of Uvedale and Tichbourne, it was denied to Wallop's followers, and any of his supporters who left the enclosure where the poll was taken were not readmitted. In polling the voters the sheriff excluded Wallop's followers on any pretext, but allowed almost all the votes of his opponents. Wallop claimed that a thousand of Tichbourne's votes were illegal, while eight hundred of his own voters were disqualified. The sheriff and his men also tallied up the vote, but did not allow Wallop to keep a count. Although polling was finally completed late in the evening, the sheriff did not add up the votes until the next morning, when he proclaimed Tichbourne and Uvedale elected. The final count was 1,673 for Tichbourne, 1,657 for Uvedale, and 1,028 for Wallop.

In view of the strenuous efforts at every step to prevent Wallop's election, it can scarcely be doubted that he was defeated by fraud. Although he carried his case to the Star Chamber, the record of its judgements in this period has been lost. But here again there was no clear issue be-

[4] P.R.O. St. Ch. 8/293:11.

tween Court and country. Both Uvedale and Tichbourne had closer connexions at Court than Wallop.

Other counties returned few leaders of the opposition. As already mentioned, Sir Anthony Cope, a strong Puritan, was elected in Oxfordshire with Sir John Croke, a supporter of the Crown. Sir Herbert Croft, representing Herefordshire, later declared that he 'was cried downe for a turne server and a turne coate' by the opposition in 1614. But the records show that he opposed the Crown, and he admitted that he had been in the opposition in 1610. Sir Samuel Sandys of Worcestershire, a brother of Sir Edwin Sandys, may well have been elected as an opponent of the Court. Sir John Holles, who sat for Nottinghamshire, was an outright opponent of the Court by 1614. Sir Roger Owen from Shropshire had been a violent member of the opposition in 1610. But aside from these few men, no prominent opposition figures were elected by the counties in 1614.[5]

There remain a few counties where contested elections had no more than local significance. In Northumberland Sir George Selby, who won the election, was excluded because he was sheriff of Durham—even though he maintained that the bishop had discharged him from that office before the election. But the sheriff of Northumberland, Ralph Selby, was accused of using trickery to elect his kinsman. On election day the sheriff called by name those voters favouring Sir George Selby and ignored the supporters of Sir Ralph Gray. As soon as he had assembled the necessary minimum of twenty-four freeholders, he declared Sir George and Sir Henry Widdeington elected and refused to take any further steps. Even though Sir George Selby was excluded and Ralph Selby suffered a

[5] B.M. Harl. MSS. 1581, ff. 356–7.

reprimand from the House of Commons, the Selby interest in Northumberland was unshaken. At a by-election to fill Sir George's place Sir William Selby was chosen.

In Cambridgeshire a bitter struggle raged between two local factions among the small county families. One faction was led by Sir John Cutts, jr., of Childerly and Sir Thomas Chichley of Wimpole; the other faction, by Sir John Cotton of Landwade and Sir John Cage. The validity of this election turned on the sheriff's refusal to take a poll. At the election Cutts and Chichley, who were supported by at least five hundred more freeholders than Cotton and Cage, were declared elected without a poll. Two hours after the election, when most of the supporters of Cutts and Chichley had returned home, Cotton demanded a poll. The sheriff refused, and his action was ultimately upheld by the House of Commons.

Social position and prestige helped close relatives of peers secure many county seats. The choice of Sir Robert Rich, the eldest son of Lord Rich, in Essex; of Sir Henry Carey, the eldest son of Lord Hunsdon, in Hertfordshire; of Sir Thomas Howard, second son of the Earl of Suffolk, in Wiltshire; and of both Henry Howard, Suffolk's third son, and Sir William Cavendish, the second son of Lord Cavendish, in Derbyshire, have been mentioned, as well as the election of Sir George Manners and Sir Peregrine Bertie, brothers of the Earl of Rutland and Lord Willoughby de Eresby, respectively, in Lincolnshire. Other heirs to peerages representing counties included Sir Mervin Audley, the eldest son of Lord Audley, in Dorset; and in Westmorland Henry, Lord Clifford, the eldest son of the Earl of Cumberland, and Sir Thomas Wharton, the eldest son of Lord Wharton. Sampson Lennard, whose son succeeded as Baron Dacre in 1612, represented

Sussex. The Earl of Pembroke found no difficulty in securing the election of a Herbert in Montgomeryshire.

In the two universities, constituencies which the Crown might hope to influence, it made a clean sweep, but not without opposition. Oxford University chose as one of its members Sir John Bennet, chancellor to Queen Anne, a master in Chancery, and a judge of the prerogative court of Canterbury. The other member was Sir Daniel Dunn, dean of the Court of Arches and also a master in Chancery. Dunn defeated Dr. Thomas James, the first librarian of the Bodleian, because of strong support from the heads of colleges despite widespread support for his opponent among the electors.

At Cambridge University the Crown succeeded in electing Sir Francis Bacon and Sir Miles Sandys, the candidate of the Earl of Northampton (Henry Howard), despite desperate attempts by the university authorities to defeat Sandys. Because Bacon was acceptable to the elements opposing Sandys, the contest was confined to the second seat. The right to elect the university's members belonged to the senate, composed of all masters of arts. But in 1614 the heads of ten houses led by Dr. Corbett, the master of Trinity Hall, attempted to gain control of the election. Failing in this manœuvre, they enlisted the aid of Dr. Duport, the deputy vice-chancellor, to elect their candidate.[6]

The candidate of Dr. Corbett and his associates was Dr. Gooch, the master of Magdalene College, who had represented the university in the parliament of 1604.

[6] Mullinger, *The University of Cambridge from the Royal Injunctions of 1535 to the Accession of Charles the First*, pp. 112, 223, 463-4; *Cambridge Antiquarian Society Communications*, iii. 203-9.

When the senate assembled on 2 April for the election, Dr. Duport, who presided, stressed the requirement that the members had to be residents of the university, a manœuvre aimed at Sandys, who was a Cambridge-shire squire and an alumnus of Cambridge, but not a resident. Duport also refused to be influenced by letters from Northampton's secretary recommending Sandys.

The voting was done by ballot. When the votes were counted, by far the largest number were for Bacon and Sandys. Gooch received seventy-four, and Dr. Corbett sixty-four. Although Dr. Duport had planned to suppress the record of Sandys's votes, the senate grew so tumultuous that he began to fear violence. Nevertheless he boldly ruled that the election of Sandys was void because he was not a resident of the university. After declaring Bacon and Gooch elected, Duport dissolved the assembly and forced his way out with some difficulty, aided by the beadles.

But the discontented masters were far from giving up the struggle. They seized the ballots for Bacon and Sandys from the registrar, and remained for some time in the regent house debating a course of action. Finally a large number of them went to King's College, where in the name of the doctors, masters, and scholars they signed a certificate of the election of Bacon and Sandys. They persuaded the sheriff to accept this certificate and return their candidates. Dr. Duport was forced to certify the election of his candidates in an irregular manner without the participation of the sheriff.

Despite Dr. Duport's protest the election of Bacon and Sandys was accepted by the House of Commons. Since there is no mention of an election contest, official pressure was probably exerted to persuade Duport and his associates to drop the matter. As in Norfolk the Crown candidate had popular support, and trickery was the only weapon available to defeat him. In both cases the sheriff was the key figure. He caused Rich's defeat in Norfolk, and Sandys's victory at Cambridge University.

In the City of London, perhaps the most important constituency in the kingdom, the Crown encountered considerable opposition. According to contemporary nomenclature, the first two of the City's four members were its knights, and the other two were its burgesses. The Crown nominated Sir Henry Montague, the recorder of London and one of the City's knights in the parliament of 1604. Since 1611 he had been the king's serjeant. On 28 February the City elected Sir Thomas Lowe as its first knight, but rejected Montague. Their first burgess was Nicholas Fuller, an opponent of the Crown in the previous parliament, while the fourth seat went to Mr. Toursom. Germain Marsham, a London letter-writer, said on 4 March that Lowe had been chosen Speaker. He added that the City had rejected Montague, and that someone else would be chosen in his place.[7]

The first round, then, went decisively against the government. Not only was Montague rejected, but also the uncompromising Fuller had secured a seat. Marsham's puzzling reference to Lowe as the choice for Speaker is the key to the ultimate solution. If he was the Speaker-designate when the London election took place, as seems probable, the City may well have objected to having both its knights spokesmen of the Crown. Probably the government persuaded the corporation to elect Monta-

---

[7] *Letters of Chamberlain*, i. 515–16; *H.M.C. Downshire MSS.* iv. 325 (Trumbull papers).

gue by dropping Lowe as Speaker. This manœuvre would account for the fact that Ranulph Crew, the Speaker, sat for the obscure government pocket-borough of Saltash, especially if he replaced Lowe as Speaker-designate at the last minute. Chamberlain did not report until 17 March that Crew was to be Speaker.[8]

At any rate the Crown had its way in the end, and Montague was elected one of the City's knights. For some unknown reason Toursom was replaced by Robert Middleton, the brother of both Sir Thomas Middleton, lord mayor 1613–14, and of Sir Hugh Middleton, the projector of the New River Company and the member for Denbighshire in 1614.

Many cases of Court influence in parliamentary boroughs in 1614 have been found. The first in point of time was the city of Rochester. As early as 13 February, a few days before a new parliament was decided on, the mayor wrote a letter to Somerset allowing him to choose one member. Sir Robert Mansell forwarded this letter to Somerset on 23 February, enclosing a letter of his own. He told Somerset that he would have been granted the nomination of both members, had Rochester not been approached by several gentlemen who were still contending over the second place.[9]

The first seat at Rochester went to Sir Edward Hoby, a seasoned courtier, who was doubtless Somerset's nominee. But Mansell's letter had a deeper motive than appeared. As treasurer of the navy he must have had much influence in Rochester, and he was canvassing for Sir Edwin Sandys in Kent. Probably he foresaw Sandys's defeat in the county and wished to reserve a seat at Rochester for him.

---

[8] *Letters of Chamberlain*, i. 517–19.
[9] P.R.O. S.P. Dom. 14/76:21; B.M. Cott. MSS. Titus B vii, ff. 465–6.

Sandys, who did lose in the county, was chosen for the second place at Rochester. Despite a comparatively wide franchise extending to all freemen, Rochester was completely under official influence in 1614.[10]

Cambridge borough was a constituency with a much narrower franchise, the electorate being limited to eight members of the corporation. But when Lord Chancellor Ellesmere, the high steward of Cambridge, wrote to the corporation wishing to nominate one of its members, the mayor answered that Sir Robert Hitcham, the Queen's attorney-general and the counsel for Cambridge, wanted one seat. Furthermore, the corporation wanted to elect Francis Brakin, their recorder, as one member and a resident of the town as the other. Nevertheless they promised to carry out Ellesmere's wishes. He must have been satisfied with Hitcham, who held one seat, while Brakin held the other.[11]

The borough of Leicester as a Duchy town was under Sir Thomas Parry's influence, but the Earl of Huntingdon, who lived at Ashby-de-la-Zouch near by, was also influential. Furthermore, a spirit of independence had grown up within the town, which was beginning to resent outside interference in parliamentary elections. The first candidate in the field was Sir William Hericke, who had been chosen at a by-election in 1605. He recommended Francis Harvey, the recorder of Leicester, for the other seat. Meanwhile the Earl of Huntingdon had made recommendations for both seats. His candidates were his brother George Hastings and his cousin Sir Henry Rich, a son of Lord Rich and a favourite of the King. Rich, whose defeat in Norfolk has been mentioned,

[10] Smith, *Rochester in Parliament*, p. 12.
[11] Cooper, *Annals of Cambridge*, iii. 60–61.

had been elected at Leicester in 1610 on Huntingdon's recommendation.[12]

The corporation hoped to solve its problem by offering one seat to George Hastings and the other to Harvey. But they feared to alienate the Earl of Huntingdon because then he might use his influence against a new charter which the corporation was seeking for the Leicester almshouse. At this point the town escaped from one dilemma only to land directly in another. Huntingdon informed them that his brother would be elected for Leicestershire, but he still demanded the election of Rich. Now it seemed as if the corporation was free to choose Rich and Harvey. But belatedly Parry exercised his traditional right, and nominated Henry Felton. Once more the town had three candidates for two seats plus the still insistent Hericke.

The recorder now stepped in to solve the problem. He refused to stand, and suggested that the corporation should consult Huntingdon about Parry's request. If the earl abandoned Rich, then Hericke would be a suitable candidate. The result was a foregone conclusion. Huntingdon continued to support Rich, and the corporation dared not flout Parry for fear of losing the almshouse charter. At the last minute Felton was unable to stand, so Parry substituted Sir Francis Leigh, a son-in-law of Lord Chancellor Ellesmere. Rich and Leigh were duly chosen on 2 April. The town also wrote to Hericke, advising him to secure Parry's support if he wanted to represent the borough in the next parliament.

[12] Thompson, *History of Leicester from the Time of the Romans to the End of the Seventeenth Century*, pp. 326, 342, 344; Stocks and Stevenson (eds.), *Records of the Borough of Leicester*, iv. 137 (Hall papers unbound, A, Nos. 57 and 89), 147–9 (Hall papers unbound, A, Nos. 74 and 78); Nichols, *History and Antiquities of the County of Leicester*, i, pt. ii, pp. 341, 425.

Perhaps the most heavy-handed case of interference in an election was Parry's action at Stockbridge, which caused his expulsion from parliament. The case was simple. Even though Stockbridge was a Duchy town with only twenty-eight electors, Parry was unable to influence their choice. A candidate named St. John received twenty-one votes, and Sir Richard Gifford received twenty-two. While Sir Walter Cope, the master of the wards, had some support in the town, Parry's other nominee, Sir Henry Wallop, was not even mentioned. Parry used official pressure to try to secure the election of his candidates. He wrote threatening letters to the town, and several voters who did not follow his advice were arrested. He also managed to frighten Gifford into declining his seat for fear of revenge. But failing to secure the necessary votes for his nominees, in the end Parry simply instructed the bailiff to insert the names of Cope and Wallop on the writ. Although Cope's return was defended on the ground that Gifford had declined, the House of Commons ordered a new election for both seats. Even though Parry was a privy councillor, he was expelled from parliament for his part in the affair.

Parry as chancellor of the Duchy of Lancaster had influence in many other boroughs both in Lancashire and elsewhere, for the Duchy property was scattered over England. In 1614 courtiers and officials secured seats in many of these boroughs. Lancashire itself gave one seat to Sir Thomas Gerrard, a courtier. The borough of Lancaster elected two Fanshawes, father and son, both Duchy officials. Edward Mosley, the attorney-general of the Duchy, sat for Preston, while Edward Wymarke, an obscure courtier, was chosen at Liverpool. Although Clement Coke, Sir Edward's choleric son, sat for

Clitheroe, he probably owed his seat to Sir Gilbert Hoghton, a courtier and neighbouring magnate. But in Newton and Wigan (where a Gerrard of a different family was elected) no Court candidates were chosen.

Outside Lancashire, Wymarke may have owed his election at Newcastle-under-Lyme, another Duchy town, to Parry. Here Robert Needham, the other member and the son of a courtier, was probably Parry's nominee also. Wymarke was elected for Peterborough as well, perhaps through the influence of Thomas Dove, the politically minded bishop. At East Grinstead, another Duchy town, Sir George Rivers, a minor official, was elected. Monmouth, also a Duchy town, chose as its single member Sir Robert Johnson, an officer in the ordnance. Henry Binge, one of the members for Sudbury, a Duchy town, was a minor legal official. Although there were several Duchy boroughs in Yorkshire, Duchy influence was weak. At Knaresborough one member was William Beecher, an official, but the other member belonged to a family of local magnates. Sir Thomas Posthumous Hoby, an old courtier, sat for Ripon, but he probably owed his seat to the Archbishop of York, who was influential in the borough. No courtier or official secured a seat at Aldborough or Boroughbridge. At Huntingdon, a Duchy town, the Cromwell influence was probably responsible for the choice of an official and a courtier. Two other Duchy towns, Higham Ferrers and Thetford, remained outside Parry's influence. But in all, he had some part in the choice of fourteen members.

The Earl of Northampton (Henry Howard), Lord Warden of the Cinque Ports, took pains to influence the choice of their 'barons' in parliament. On 28 February 1614 he wrote to the mayor of Hythe asserting his

'ancient privilege' to nominate one member from each of
the ports. As soon as the writ was received, Lionel Cranfield, Northampton's candidate, was elected without
opposition. At Dover, where both members were officials
of Dover Castle, the Lord Warden secured both seats. Sir
Arthur Ingram, the capitalist-courtier, sat for Romney.
Thomas Watson, a teller of the Exchequer, was Northampton's nominee at Rye. But as the other member, Edward Hendon, became a serjeant in 1616, he may have
been Northampton's candidate also. Winchelsea was a
similar case. One member was the captain of Deal Castle,
and the other had formerly been in Northampton's service. Sir Thomas Smyth, who sat for Sandwich, was a
fiscal official of the Crown. Only in Hastings did Northampton fail to secure a seat.

The Howards also had influence in a number of other
boroughs. Thomas Hitchcock was Northampton's nominee at Bishop's Castle. At Portsmouth, where Northampton's rival the Earl of Pembroke was governor, Northampton nevertheless secured the election of John Griffith,
his secretary. Lord Howard of Effingham, the son of the
Lord Admiral, the Earl of Nottingham, was lord of the
manor of Bletchingley. The borough obediently elected
Sir John Trevor, Nottingham's secretary, and Sir Charles
Howard, jr., Nottingham's nephew. Nottingham himself
was the lord of Reigate, which elected his son Sir Edward
Howard and John Suckling, a courtier and official, the
father of the poet.

The Earl of Arundel (Thomas Howard) was the lord
of Bramber, and most of its voters were his tenants. Sir
John Leeds, a courtier, was probably his candidate in
1614. Arundel also dominated Horsham, where Sir
Thomas Vavasor, knight marshal of the Household, was

elected in 1614. Perhaps the colourful Sir Thomas Shirley was Arundel's nominee in Steyning in 1614. Thomas Howard, the Earl of Suffolk, Arundel's uncle, shared political influence in Dunwich with Sir Edward Coke. In 1614 Henry Dade was elected at the request of Suffolk while Philip Gawdy was elected by Coke's influence.

In Cornwall Crown influence appeared in many boroughs. Camelford returned George Cotton, a brother of the Bishop of Exeter, and Robert Naunton, a clerk in the secretary's office. Edward Leech and Sir Henry Vane, both officials, sat for Lostwithiel. St. Mawes elected Francis Vivian, captain of the castle, and Sir Nicholas Smith, a customs official. The Speaker, Ranulph Crew, and Sir Robert Phelips, son of the master of the rolls, represented Saltash. The strongly royalist Killigrew family held seats in Helston, Penryn, and St. Ives, though probably their success was due to their own influence. Courtiers, minor officials, and officers of the Duchy of Cornwall also gained seats at Bossiney, Launceston, Liskeard, East and West Looe, Newport, Penryn, Tregony, and Truro. Of the forty Cornish borough seats for which returns have been found, the Crown had twenty supporters.

The Earl of Pembroke, the head of the Herbert family and a leader of the Protestant faction in the council, had influence in a number of boroughs. Since 1600 he had been lord of the manor of Shaftesbury and a large landowner in the borough. In 1614 he secured the election there of Henry Croke, the son of a judge of the King's Bench. Even in this period Old Sarum had achieved that state of decay which was the wonder of later generations. Control in 1614 was shared by the Earls of Salisbury and Pembroke, but Pembroke had the greater influence. William Price, his agent in Glamorganshire, was his nominee in 1614, but the other member, William Ravenscroft, a minor official, owed his seat to Pembroke or Salisbury.

At Wilton, the home of the Pembrokes, both members were the earl's nominees. One, Thomas Morgan, was his steward. The other, Sir Robert Sidney, was the heir of Viscount Lisle, a prominent courtier. At Downton Gilbert Raleigh, a kinsman of Sir Walter, may have owed his seat to Pembroke, who supported Raleigh's projects. William Kent, Pembroke's chief steward, sat for Devizes. Although Pembroke was lord of Cardiff, in 1614 its member was a lawyer apparently not connected with the Herberts. Of the thirty-two Wiltshire members, seventeen were followers of Pembroke or had other Court connexions.

Lord Knollys, likewise a privy councillor, exercised influence in a group of four boroughs in 1614. As high steward of Oxford he nominated Sir John Ashley. He was also high steward of Reading, where his nephew Robert Knollys and Francis Moore, a legal supporter of the Crown, were elected. Abingdon's single member was his brother Sir Robert Knollys. At Wallingford he nominated William Reynolds.[13]

Gatton, which, like Old Sarum, was already decayed in the early Stuart period, was under the control of the council after 1584. The council's nominee in 1614 was probably Sir John Brooke, a follower of the Earl of Dunfermline, lord chancellor of Scotland and a member of the English privy council. After 1571 the council also had a seat available at Poole. In 1614 it went to Sir Thomas Walsingham, jr., whose father, a well-known figure at Court, defeated Sir Edwin Sandys in Kent. Haslemere was created a parliamentary borough in 1584

[13] Hedges, *History of Wallingford*, ii. 200, 242.

to provide seats for Court supporters. In 1614 one of its members was Sir William Brown, who had served in the Low Countries and had been lieutenant-governor of Flushing.

At Dorchester, where the Duke of Lennox was high steward, Francis Ashley, a legal supporter of the Crown, was chosen. Lord Chancellor Ellesmere was high steward of St. Albans, where the Crown secured both seats. One went to Sir Francis Bacon, who, however, chose to sit for Cambridge University, and the other to Henry Finch, a legal supporter of the Crown.

Sir Edward Coke secured the election of his son Sir Robert at Coventry. Sir Edward Phelips, the master of the rolls, controlled a seat at Taunton, which went to John Dunn, whose father was an ecclesiastical lawyer and judge. The borough of Northampton was a supreme example of family influence coupled with official position. The mecca of English non-conformists and a centre for the production of Marprelate pamphlets, it had been represented repeatedly by Peter Wentworth in the latter part of Elizabeth's reign. In 1604 Sir Henry Yelverton, whose family influence was strong in Northampton, was elected. Although he deserted the opposition during the parliament of 1604 and became solicitor-general in 1613, he was again elected in 1614, carrying his brother-in-law Francis Beale with him. Here a traditional alignment fell before family influence.

A few boroughs showed a mixture of political alignment, all, interestingly enough, involving James Whitelocke, a well-known opposition leader. In 1614 Corfe Castle was under the control of Lady Hatton, the ill-matched wife of Lord Chief Justice Coke and a daughter of the Earl of Exeter. Here she nominated John Dackome, an official close to the first Earl of Salisbury, and James Whitelocke. When Whitelocke chose to sit for Woodstock, she replaced him with Sir Thomas Tracy, a royal official. Sir Robert Killigrew, a strong royalist, controlled both seats at Helston. He occupied one himself and gave the other to Whitelocke, who nominated his brother-in-law. In Woodstock, where Whitelocke was the recorder, he contested a seat against the Earl of Montgomery, the steward of the manor and a favourite of the King. Although Whitelocke defeated Montgomery's nominee, the other seat went to a courtier.[14]

In a few boroughs the Crown encountered difficulties. Although the Earl of Northampton wrote to Totnes as early as 20 February, the corporation replied that they had promised one seat to their recorder, and wished to elect one resident member. Although they asked the recorder to forgo his privilege, he stood firm, assuring them that his nominee would please Northampton. The recorder named Nathaniel Rich, certainly no friend of the Spanish faction, while the second member was a merchant of Totnes. Northampton also asked to nominate one member at Dartmouth, but the corporation refused. Both members were local merchants, one of whom by coincidence was named Thomas Howard.

Sir Robert Hitcham, the Queen's attorney-general, and Sir Henry Spelman, a courtier, tried to secure election at King's Lynn. But the corporation rejected them on the pretext that a statute of 1413 forbade the election of non-residents. One seat went to the mayor, and the other to their recorder, who was also a local merchant.[15]

The most peculiar case of election trickery was the

[14] *Liber Famelicus of Sir James Whitelocke*, pp. 40–41.
[15] B.M. Add. MSS. 24346, f. 31.

borough of Carmarthen. In Welsh boroughs the single burgess was elected at the shire-town with the smaller towns of the county participating. A Mr. Thomas was chosen, but the sheriff refused to make the return because the writ required a burgess to be returned *de burgo vocat' l'Shire-town*, and no town in Carmarthenshire was named 'Shire-town'! What lay behind this strange interpretation is not clear, and no record remains of the final result.[16]

Two questions remain to be considered: whether or not the election was a defeat for the Crown; and to what extent the parliament was packed. In regard to the first question, the traditional view, given by Gardiner and repeated by Tanner, is that the Court candidates were 'everywhere rejected'. Even though evidence points to the opposite conclusion, this concept of the election as a contest between Court and country is fundamentally unsound. In 1614 England was far from being divided into two political camps on the issue of royal policies. Such a concept carries political ideas of the nineteenth and twentieth centuries back into a period when these ideas did not exist. While England's political consciousness made great strides between 1621 and 1649, in 1614 it was still dormant. No single case has been found of a clear-cut contest between the Court faction and the popular faction in 1614.[17]

On the contrary there are a number of examples which show a complete confusion in alliance. Men had no hesitation about changing their colours from one place to another. The Earl of Rutland supported Sir Robert Phelips, a Court candidate, in Somerset. But in Lincoln-

---

[16] *Commons jn.* i. 461 (12 Apr. 1614).
[17] Gardiner, *History of England*, ii. 229–31; Tanner, *English Constitutional Conflicts of the Seventeenth Century*, pp. 46–47.

shire, Rutland backed his brother against Sir Thomas Monson, a royal official. Thomas Mansell, the treasurer of the navy, canvassed Kent for Sir Edwin Sandys, the opposition leader in 1614, against a courtier. When Sandys lost in Kent, Mansell secured a seat for him at Rochester. In Hampshire Sir Henry Wallop stood against two candidates with connexions at Court. But when he failed, he secured a seat through a privy councillor. Lady Hatton offered a seat to James Whitelocke, a leading opposition figure. When he chose another constituency, she replaced him with a courtier. Sir Robert Killigrew, a staunch royalist, also offered a seat to Whitelocke, and accepted his brother-in-law as the member. An understanding of the 1614 election requires the substitution of personalities for political parties. In 1604 the Court made little preparation for the election, and the official group fell below normal; in 1614 the Crown simply tried to retrieve its position and secure more seats for its followers.

The answers to the questions posed are now apparent. The election was not a defeat for the Crown. On the contrary the official and Court element was somewhat stronger than usual, and few of this element who desired seats were denied them. The Crown did not seek a majority of pliable members who would obey its will without protest. It simply wished to have many of its servants in the House, those who understood its policies and were sympathetic towards them. This group would provide the nucleus around which a heterogeneous group of rural gentry could be stabilized, so that the business of government could be conducted. In this sense parliament was packed, but in no other. An analysis of the House of Commons in the next chapter shows that its composition was quite normal. But the resentment of the gentry at 'interference' in local elections found tumultuous expression during the session. The result was to discredit the Crown and to weaken fatally the influence of the official leadership.

Chapter IV

The New House of Commons

THE House of Commons in 1614 is usually characterized as a body of new men, young, inexperienced, and excitable. During the session itself the report was current that over 300 members out of 464 had never sat in parliament before. Bacon, writing to the King in 1615, set the proportion of new members at three-quarters, or about 356.[1]

Actually the number of inexperienced members was 281, against 183 who had sat in parliament before. Contemporaries overstated the proportion of new members. Of these 281 new members 144 saw service in later parliaments, while 137 served only in 1614. The proportion of new members was 61 per cent. According to Neale in Elizabethan parliaments about 50 per cent. were usually new members. But Elizabethan parliaments met at frequent intervals. The only two general elections comparable to 1614 were 1571, the first in nearly eight years, and 1584, the first in over twelve years. In 1571 62 per cent. were new members, while the figure was 70 per cent. in 1584. A similar comparison can be made with the Long Parliament. If the Short Parliament is disregarded, 59 per cent. of the members of the Long Parliament were new men. Consequently the percentage of new members in 1614 was about average if the ten-year break since 1604 is considered. Likewise the proportion of new members in 1614 who served in later parliaments is slightly higher than the usual Elizabethan percentage. It is quite clear

---

[1] *Commons jn.* i. 467, 473; Spedding, *Letters and Life of Bacon*, v. 176–91.

that the parliament of 1614 did not deviate from the normal pattern in the number of inexperienced members.[2]

The parliament of 1614 is also regarded as lacking the usual group of royal officials. Actually the reverse was true. In this respect it was probably more typical than the parliament of 1604, in which the official element was weak. While four privy councillors were elected in 1614, there were only two in the lower House during most of the parliament of 1604. For a time early in 1606 Sir John Herbert was the only privy councillor in the Commons. Not until 1610 did the number of councillors in that parliament rise to three, their effective strength in 1614 after the expulsion of Sir Thomas Parry.

There were also many other members of the lower House in 1614 who had Court connexions. They included 6 important officials like the attorney-general and the solicitor-general, an ambassador, and an Irish privy councillor. There were also 22 legal supporters, among whom were numbered several serjeants and masters of requests, as well as the attorneys-general of the Queen and the Duchy, the Prince's solicitor, and two important officials in ecclesiastical courts. Officials of lesser rank, who numbered 32, served in such varied departments as the exchequer, the jewel house, the customs, the ordnance, the mint, the court of wards, the naval administration, the secretary's office, the petty bag, and the Duchy of Cornwall. Courtiers and petty or ceremonial officials like gentleman of the privy chamber, carver to the King, and the King's cupbearer numbered 65. Close relatives of officials held 25 seats, and 6 more seats went to miscellaneous royal supporters. The total of this whole group

[2] Neale, *Elizabethan House of Commons*, p. 309; Brunton and Pennington, *Members of the Long Parliament*, p. 189.

reached the substantial figure of 160 out of 464 members. The House of Commons in 1614 was unusual because it contained more officials and courtiers instead of fewer.[3]

In occupation and social status the House of Commons followed the general pattern of the later Elizabethan parliaments. If the members are classified on broad lines according to their principal interests, we find that 208 were gentry or the sons of gentry. Another 17 belonged to the families of peers or were their dependents. Professional officials numbered 50, exactly equalling the number of courtiers. Lawyers outnumbered merchants 48 to 42, while the House contained one soldier and one doctor of medicine. The only significant variation from the figures given by Neale for the parliament of 1584 is an increase in the official and Court element.[4]

Likewise the number of members having higher education remained constant. Members with a university education numbered 65, and members educated at the inns of court numbered 49, while 138 others had attended both. The total with higher education came to 252, exactly the same as the figure for the parliament of 1593. But there had been some detailed changes. Although a few more members had attended Oxford in preference to Cambridge in 1593, the parliament of 1614 overwhelmingly preferred Oxford. Of 203 members with a university education, 135 had attended Oxford, but only 68 had attended Cambridge. As Cambridge was the Puritan stronghold and Oxford was becoming High Church, these figures cast a shadow of doubt on the strength of Puritanism in the Addled Parliament.[5]

[3] See Appendix IV for a detailed list.
[4] Neale, *Elizabethan House of Commons*, pp. 301-2.
[5] Ibid., pp. 302-3.

Although the House of Commons in 1614 did not vary significantly from its Elizabethan counterparts, by 1640 there were marked changes in the Commons. The Long Parliament included more sons of peers and gentry, and the number of lawyers and merchants had increased significantly. On the other hand, the number of courtiers and professional officials fell from 100 in 1614 to 49 in 1640. The total membership with official and Court connexions had also dropped, but less drastically, from 160 out of 464 to about 125 out of 547.

The members of the Long Parliament were also better educated than the members of the Addled Parliament. The number of university men increased by over 100, and the number of members educated at the inns of court nearly doubled. It is significant that in the Long Parliament the number of Cambridge men nearly doubled while the Oxford men increased only slightly.[6]

While the differences between the House of Commons in 1614 and the same body in 1640 are indicative of the changing political climate, the Addled Parliament still followed the Elizabethan pattern in its composition. Consequently the causes of its utter failure must be sought elsewhere. While a general consideration of these causes will be reserved for a later stage, one factor becomes obvious when the membership is analysed. One great weakness of this parliament was incompetent leadership. However brilliant individual members of a legislative body may be, they must be organized and guided if they are to avoid futility.

Among the supporters of the Crown, the nominal leaders were inexperienced. The secretary of state, Sir Ralph Winwood, had never sat in parliament before, and

[6] Keeler, *The Long Parliament*, pp. 17-18, 21-23, 27-28.

the speaker, Ranulph Crew, had been a member only in 1593. Other important officials or leading figures like Caesar, Yelverton, Bacon, Neville, and Wotton, gave the royal cause little support. The burden fell on more obscure figures like Sir Henry Montague, Sir George More, and Francis Ashley. They tried to increase their influence over the House by ceaseless activity, but they never succeeded in wielding the authority which belonged to their inactive superiors. On the whole the royal supporters lacked unity, experience, and initiative. Again and again control slipped from their hands because they sat silent at a crucial moment. They repeatedly yielded opportunities to the opposition by default, and the opposition was quick to seize its advantages.

The opposition leaders were a diverse group. Some, like Sir Edwin Sandys and Sir Dudley Digges, were well-connected men who might have been expected to support the Crown. As a matter of fact, there was much shifting from one side to the other. Shortly before the Addled Parliament met, Digges was seeking employment at Court, and Bacon reported that Sandys was on the point of deserting the opposition. Also, towards the end of their lives both men were reconciled to the Crown.[7]

Other opposition leaders like Nicholas Fuller, John Hoskyns, and Christopher Brooke, were connected with the commercial and legal classes. The legalistic aspect of political disputes in this period owed much of its character to the lawyers in the lower House and to the legal education of many other members.

Another opposition element was drawn from the landed gentry of established local families, important in

---

[7] McClure (ed.), *Letters of John Chamberlain*, i. 514-15; Spedding, *Letters and Life of Bacon*, iv. 365, 370.

their own counties but not well known outside them. Sir Roger Owen, Sir Herbert Croft, and Sir John Savile were representative of this group. Although some opposition leaders in 1614 were undoubtedly Puritans, Puritanism was not the common element of the opposition that it later became. But a large section of the Commons was in agreement on important questions in dispute even in 1614. Both merchants and gentry attacked impositions. Indeed everyone was reluctant to vote supply until reforms had been made. After only ten years on the throne the King had alienated most of the important elements in English society.

But in 1614 the opposition leaders had not learned to make their weight felt. To some degree they suffered from the same defects as the supporters of the Crown. The parliament of 1614 formed a hiatus between two periods of parliamentary development. From the 1580's through 1604 a constant series of new parliaments made it possible for younger men to enter a House dominated by older and wiser leaders. The five parliaments of the 1620's provided the opportunity for real leadership to develop. But the parliament of 1614 was isolated from both chains of development. Inexperienced leaders attempted to control an untried House. While they could conduct a controversial matter well enough at first, the smooth course of events was easily disturbed. The House reacted violently to any curb, and the opposition leaders found themselves powerless to check its headlong course. Although they might plead for moderation, they could not control the forces which they themselves had loosed.

The King never gained a practical understanding of legislative machinery. He did not realize that in parliament as in everything else experience was necessary for smooth and efficient operation. A new House of Commons could not be expected to conduct itself soberly and effectively under inexperienced leadership.

Chapter V

The House of Lords

IN 1614 the House of Lords was still a small body made up almost entirely of bishops, earls, and barons. Of the 84 lay peers only the Marquess of Winchester held a higher title than earl, although the Earl of Richmond was the Duke of Lennox in Scotland. There were 27 earls and 54 barons in the House, but only two viscounts. The lords spiritual included the 2 archbishops and the 24 English and Welsh bishops. The total membership of the House of Lords was 110, including 3 minors.[1]

In 1614 exactly one-half of the peerage had been ennobled since the death of Henry VIII. Sixteen peers held titles granted prior to 1300. Eight held fourteenth-century titles. Seven held titles granted between 1401 and 1485, but not a single noble family in 1614 had entered the House of Lords under Henry VII. Eleven peers owed their original creations to Henry VIII. Although there were twelve peerages dating from Edward VI and Mary, Elizabeth's creations numbered only eight. But in ten years James I had created twenty-two new peers. In 1614 there were two Scots (Richmond and Somerset) in the House of Lords. The Earl of Oxford held the oldest title, dating from 1142, but the Earl of Richmond's Scottish title was nearly as old.

If promotions and restorations are considered, James I had an even greater part in creating the House of Lords in 1614. Thirty-four of the lay peers owed their titles in some way to him. He had restored to the Earl of

---

[1] For the membership of the House of Lords see Appendix II.

Southampton the title which he had lost in 1601. The Earls of Essex and Arundel and Lord Paget had been restored to titles forfeited by their fathers. The Earls of Suffolk and Exeter had been advanced from barons to the higher rank since 1603, and the Earl of Dorset's father had also been advanced from the rank of baron. The Duke of Lennox (in Scotland) had received his English earldom of Richmond from the King. The eldest sons of four earls had been summoned to the upper House in their fathers' baronies since 1603: Herbert (Worcester), Howard de Walden (Suffolk), Howard of Effingham (Nottingham), and Clinton (Lincoln). Three earls (Montgomery, Northampton, and Somerset) and Viscount Lisle owed their elevation to the peerage to the King. James had also raised the father of the Earl of Salisbury to the peerage. In addition, fifteen barons, who are listed in Appendix II, had received their titles since 1603. The fathers of two other barons, Russell and Petre, had also received their titles from James I.

Of the lords spiritual both archbishops and 14 bishops owed their elevation or promotion to the King. Of those who did not, 6 (Bangor, Carlisle, Hereford, Norwich, St. David's, and Salisbury) never took their seats in 1614. The 4 Elizabethan bishops who sat in this parliament were Exeter, Llandaff, Peterborough, and Winchester.

If attendance is considered, the recent creations outnumbered the older peerages in 1614. Only 19 peers whose creations dated before 1485 were present, while 46 newer peers sat. Even if the dividing line is placed at the death of Henry VIII, the older peerages were still in the minority by a ratio of 25 old titles to 40 new titles. The single marquess, 7 earls, 1 viscount, and 10 barons were absent in 1614. Of these, only the Earl of Arundel,

Lord Clinton, and Lord Clifton owed their titles to the King. The maximum number of members attending in 1614 was: 20 earls, 1 viscount, 44 barons, 2 archbishops, and 18 bishops, or a grand total of 85. The highest attendance at one time was 74 on 6 June 1614, the day before parliament was dissolved.

Fifteen members of the House of Lords had seats on the privy council. They included the Archbishop of Canterbury, 9 earls, and 5 barons. The archbishop, 5 of the earls, and 4 of the barons owed their titles to the King.

The dominant faction both at Court and in the House of Lords centred around the Howard family, which held six peerages in 1614. Three of its members were on the privy council. In addition, Lord Knollys and the Earl of Somerset, both privy councillors, were married to Howard women. The leading figure in the family was the Earl of Northampton, a partisan of Spain and Roman Catholicism. In alliance with Somerset, the King's favourite, Northampton had the upper hand over his chief adversaries, the Archbishop of Canterbury, Lord Chancellor Ellesmere, and the Earl of Pembroke.

In 1614 the Crown still held a dominant position in the House of Lords. This dominance was partly the result of natural advantages, but it came partly from the close bond between the Crown and the peerage. In 1614 the feudal tradition, which regarded the Lords as the personal councillors of the King, had not entirely disappeared.

The large proportion of privy councillors in the House of Lords also gave the Crown a marked advantage. In the House of Commons there were only three or four councillors out of perhaps 340 members in attendance. In the House of Lords ten or a dozen councillors were usually present in a house of 50 to 65. Even though the council suffered from internal divisions, it presented an unbroken front to the opposition in the upper House. In the absence of a well-organized system of political parties the councillors had a marked advantage.

In addition to the councillors the Crown had a firm block of supporters in the bishops, about 15 of whom were usually present. In one of the most crucial tests of the session only the Archbishop of York deserted the Crown. In the parliament of 1614 this solidarity was probably normal. The council and the bishops gave the Crown a solid block of about 27 members. With attendance normally around 65 the support of only about half a dozen other peers was enough to give the Crown a majority.

On the other hand the opposition was loosely knit, casual, and unorganized. Although its leader, the Earl of Southampton, was a brilliant man, he had many other interests. His chief concern in life was not politics, and he did not let politics interfere with his other activities. His followers supported the opposition for many different reasons, not the least of which was personal advancement. At this time few of them seem to have been moved by deep religious or political convictions. Their attendance in the House was often irregular, and their interest was wavering.

Finally, the Crown had one great advantage inseparable from politics in the early Stuart period, the support of the dominant faction at Court. When the Addled Parliament met, the Howard–Somerset alliance was firmly cemented. Despite the opposition of Abbot, Ellesmere, and Pembroke, the Spanish faction, astutely promoted by Sarmiento, the Spanish ambassador, gained a complete ascendancy at Court. Those who took part in Court life, and they were numerous among the peerage, were drawn towards the dominant element. On the other hand peers who did not frequent the Court were too ignorant of affairs of state to formulate policy. After offering what advice they could, they felt bound both by their own limitations and by their sense of loyalty to support the King's chosen councillors. Although a factious and casual opposition existed in 1614, the King could depend on the House of Lords to defend his policies and his prerogative against the encroachments of the House of Commons.

Chapter VI

The Royal Programme

DURING the elections royal officials were hard at work preparing a programme of legislation. But despite all that could be done to disguise the fact, it was perfectly apparent that the parliament had been summoned to solve the King's financial problems. Even Bacon, who believed that the real reason should be concealed, privately admitted that money was the chief end in view.[1]

The object of the royal programme, then, was to obtain a grant of supply. But the King's advisers had the difficult task of finding concessions that would satisfy the Commons without encroaching on the prerogative. They were caught between the popular demand for major reforms and the King's stubborn insistence on retaining all his powers undiminished. Furthermore, factionalism in the council made agreement difficult. Each faction tried to gain the King's ear even at the cost of betraying their associates for no more than temporary advantage.

Because Neville and his associates were the proponents of concessions to the Commons, the initiative in drafting a programme lay with them, but they were forced to leave its presentation to friends on the council. In preparation for the session a long list of bills was drawn up, debated in the council, criticized by the judges and learned counsel, and finally presented to the King for his approval.[2]

[1] B.M. Cott. MSS. Titus F iv, ff. 351–2.   [2] P.R.O. S.P.D. 14/76: 31.

But even in the weeks before parliament met, so many doubts were being cast on the influence of the undertakers (Neville and his friends) that their supporters were beginning to panic. The Earl of Suffolk (Thomas Howard), who was making a pretence of joining the Earl of Pembroke, the leader of the Protestant faction, in support of Neville and the undertakers, wrote to Somerset in March:

... the last nyght pembrook came to me in the garden speaking in broken phrases that he could not tell what would come of this parlement because he founde by the consultation last day that my lords had no greate conceite that ther wolde be any great good effected for our master, dyvers of my lords having spoken with many wyse parlament men who do generally decline from the undertakers. Only pembrook and my selfe were the hoopfull belevers of good success. Too or three petty counselors more seemed to be indeferently conceyted, but so as my lord of pembrook is much unsatisfyed that thay are no more confydent in hys friendes. . . .

All this time Suffolk was merely leading Pembroke on in order to thwart his schemes. In his letter to Somerset, Suffolk continued:

... but I must make you laugh to tell you that my lord pryvy seale [Northampton] soberly sayes to me, my lord you enclyne before the counsell to much to thes undertakers. Thys trobles me nothing, for yf we may do our master the servyse we wysh by our dessembling, I am well contented to play the knave a lytle with them. . . .[3]

Despite his devious manœuvrings, Suffolk joined with Pembroke a few days later in presenting Neville's proposals to the council. The council finally drew up four

---

[3] B.M. Cott. MSS. Titus F iv, ff. 340–1.

different lists of bills numbering fifty-eight in all as the royal legislative programme. The first list was a series of eleven bills of grace, which represented the work of Neville and the undertakers. These proposed concessions varied only slightly from Neville's earlier suggestions discussed in Chapter II. The second list, containing nine bills, was a series of measures for the good of the commonwealth drawn up by the council at the King's direction. Most of these bills were intended to deal with such secondary problems as legal fees, piracy, and dueling; but some of them, such as a bill to prevent building near London, were designed to give the force of law to royal proclamations. None of them dealt with any major grievances, and at least one, a bill to prevent inclosures, might well arouse the opposition of influential elements among the gentry.

A third section of ten bills, also the work of the council, was styled a memorandum of secret bills. Together with measures of minor importance, it included several bills representing major phases of government policy, such as the naturalization of the Count Palatine, James's son-in-law, and the plantation of Ireland. An interesting item on this list in view of later history was a bill 'for the suppressing and supply of Boroughs of Parliament according to the present state of the towns of this realm'. But again, no major problems were dealt with in this list. The final section contained twenty-eight bills not yet discussed, a hodge-podge of private bills and matters of little importance. The Crown's legislative programme as it emerged from the council was no more realistic than the earlier proposals of Neville and Bacon. It made no attempt to come to grips with the problems of the age.[4]

[4] B.M. Harl. MSS. 4289, ff. 231ᵛ-3; 6258A, ff. 45-46; B.M. Cott. MSS.

Meanwhile Bacon had drafted another proposal, but it was so fantastic that it does not seem likely that he presented it to the King. He began by attacking Neville and the undertakers.

...in the election of Knights and Burgases now to be Chosen, where there is exceptions to all those that have anie Waie a dependensy on his Majestie, by which doeinge mens affections appeares It is bruted abroad that some few gentlemen that were most opposett to his Majesty the last Parliament, for perticuler promotions will undertake to carrie this Parlament for his Majestys profit, and ends, which other men of their like Rancke and qualitie doth so much conteme and scorne, and takes for so great an Iniurie to themselves, and the Parlament house, as that they begin to bandy, and to make a faction which is like to breake forth to open discontent at their sitting.

If theis few gentlemens estates, their callings, their deserts in the common wealthe, and peoples estimations of them, be truly examined, I thinke they cann assume little to themselves, to challenge such prerogative above others of better Ranke and quallitie. But especiallie they thinke to Commannd the tonge, harte, and consciences, of those that are strangers to them, dwelling in farr shiers, and remote places, where perhaps their names have not been so much as heard of amongst them. And therefore it is strange to me, that men will so undertake to carrie a Parlament, before they shall knowe whoe shalbe elected into the house, or whether their propotitions wilbe acceptable unto them yea, or no. . . . The ground I perceave they have to worke uppon is the ventures that shall proceed from his Majesty, in the release of his wards, The office of Alienation, and some other greevances, All which have been often reitterated in the last Parliament. . . .[5]

Titus F iv, f. 345; P.R.O. S.P.D. 14/74:46. For a complete list of these bills see Appendix VII.   [5] B.M. Cott. Titus F iv, ff. 351–2.

After declaring that the undertakers would do more harm than good, Bacon went on to propose a unique method for handling grievances and supply. The King should appoint a commission of the lord lieutenant and the leading gentry in each shire to negotiate with the persons of quality in their own county for the redress of grievances in return for a grant of money. Then each shire should send two or three gentlemen before the council to make a final bargain. After such an agreement had been made in every shire, parliament could do nothing but acquiesce. This proposal indicates that Bacon was completely out of touch with English political life. It is difficult to see how he could have believed that the people would consent to the practical abolition of parliament, or that they would co-operate in a scheme transparently designed to overthrow the traditional constitution. If this proposal really reflects his political theories, he would have been no more successful than the King in managing parliament.

Bacon performed a more practical service by presenting a memorial to the King with suggestions for his opening speech to parliament. The central theme of this memorial was that the King should not bargain with his subjects like a merchant. He should simply expect them to relieve his wants because of their natural affection for the Crown. He should begin by stating that parliament had been summoned to give counsel and consent to important national problems, not to bargain or indulge in endless orations.[6]

After this introduction Bacon advised the King to explain why he had summoned parliament. He should declare that the main reason was to naturalize the Count

[6] Spedding, *Letters and Life of Bacon*, v. 24–30.

Palatine and his issue. Then he should mention the financial problem, dwelling on the extraordinary peace-time drain on his finances, and on the dangers of an empty treasury. But he should not give details of the financial situation, and he should not offer concessions or make threats.

Bacon then suggested that the King should promise bills of grace at the beginning of the session and a general pardon at its conclusion. The bills of grace were intended to anticipate the complaints of the Commons. The King should then state that he would confer with parliament on other problems when all these matters had been settled. In a significant marginal note Bacon declared that this reference was intended to raise the hope of an agreement on impositions.

In the next section, the King should explain how he meant to deal with parliament. In the last parliament he had bargained like a merchant, and the Commons had haggled like contractors. But in this parliament he would act the part of a gracious King, relying on the love of his subjects.

Bacon advised the King to have a separate bill for each grievance. In this way one bill would not be delayed while new provisions for other grievances were added. The King should promise the Commons free access to ask for additional graces, and he should deal directly with them instead of through conferences between the two Houses. He should ask for a short and harmonious session, with the promise of another session to follow.

In the last part of his speech the King should declare that he would not abandon any of his lawful powers, but he would not extend his prerogative at the expense of his subjects. He should also say that while he could meet his financial obligations by selling Crown property and by economizing, he preferred to depend on the affection of the Commons.

The King should caution the Commons not to believe rumours of undertaking. He should state that he relied on the whole lower House, rather than on a few individuals. In his peroration he should declare his affection for parliament.

Despite his earlier suggestions to the contrary, in this memorandum Bacon advised the King to admit his financial difficulties and ask for a grant of supply. In his earlier memorandum Bacon had suggested that the supply question should be allowed to arise naturally, and he had even declared that it was better to end a session harmoniously without a grant of supply than to ask for subsidies. But by 1614 the King's financial plight could not be concealed. Even the feeble suggestion that the King could increase his revenue out of his own resources was not convincing. Although Bacon still advocated an approach based on loyalty instead of one based on a bargaining spirit, he had to admit that financial necessity was the real reason for summoning parliament.

It is significant that Bacon advised the King to deny rumours of undertaking at the very beginning of the session. The persistence of these rumours gives rise to the suspicion that the Spanish faction was using them to embroil the King and the Commons even before parliament met. Bacon's memorandum was well received by the King, and in his speeches to parliament on 5 April and 9 April James drew heavily on Bacon's suggestions.

The choice of a new secretary of state was the final step in the preparations for parliament. Of the four serious candidates Sir Henry Wotton had been discredited before the end of 1612 when the King learned of his witty epigram written in Augsburg in 1604: 'An ambassador is an honest man sent to lie abroad for the good of his country.' By early 1614 Lake, the Howard candidate, had likewise fallen into the background partly because of his own ineptness and partly because of suspicions that he was a Papist. Consequently the race had narrowed to Winwood and Neville. Although Winwood seemed to be on the brink of success in February of 1614, his appointment failed to materialize. His failure at this time arose from the machinations of the Howards. Despairing of Lake's hopes, they threw their influence behind Neville partly to cause dissension between him and Winwood, partly to stir up trouble in the Commons through rumours of undertaking, and partly to secure a good position for Lake as their price for dropping Neville. Although Neville was crippled by gout and corpulence, the Howards convinced such influential figures as the Earl of Pembroke, the Earl of Southampton, and Lord Sheffield that he would be appointed despite Somerset's support of Winwood.[7]

Finally, on 29 March, after a delay of almost two years, Winwood became the principal secretary of state. Lake was made a privy councillor without receiving any other office, while Neville refused the position of treasurer of the chamber. So the issue was settled at last, but too late to be of much advantage. The fact that the appointment was made only seven days before parliament met gave rise to the suspicion that it had been done to influence the Commons.

[7] H.M.C. Downshire MSS. iv. 318-19, 340-1 (Trumbull papers); Letters of Chamberlain, i. 507, 509-10, 515-16, 521; P.R.O. S.P.D. 14/76: 34; P.R.O. S.P. Venice 99/15, f. 213; P.R.O. Spanish transcripts 12/35 (Sarmiento to Philip III, 30 Apr./9 May 1614); B.M. Cott. MSS. Titus F iv, ff. 340-1.

The new secretary of state had a broad background of experience in diplomatic affairs, but no experience at all in parliament. Born about 1563, he had been well educated at Oxford University, where he spent the years 1577–92, serving as a proctor in the latter year. Soon after his term as proctor, he left the university and made an extensive tour of the Continent.

When Winwood returned to England, his accomplishments were recognized by the Earl of Essex. In 1599 through Essex's influence he became secretary to Sir Henry Neville, the ambassador to France and his rival for the post of secretary of state in 1614. Neville, who spent much of his time in England, was dismissed in 1601 under suspicion of complicity in the Essex rebellion. Winwood performed many of Neville's duties in his absence and succeeded him as ambassador in 1601. Returning to England briefly in 1603, Winwood was next appointed English agent in Holland. Here he remained for some years engaged in diplomatic affairs, despite his desire to return home and settle down to a quiet country life near his old friend Neville. When he finally did come back to England in 1613, it was only to become secretary of state, a post which he held until his death in 1617.

Although Winwood's appointment as secretary was a concession to public opinion, he was suspected of having paid hard cash for Somerset's support. Also he had powerful enemies. Lake, Caesar, Herbert, and other officials were jealous of the new secretary. Winwood's hatred of Spain and Roman Catholicism made him the enemy of the powerful Howard family even though this attitude did gain him some popularity in the House of Commons. In addition his interest in the reform of ecclesiastical abuses alienated the higher clergy, who suspected him of Puritanism.

Winwood laboured under a threefold disadvantage in dealing with the House of Commons. In the first place, he became secretary so shortly before parliament met that he had no time to prepare for the session. The extensive preparations already detailed had been made by others and were thrust upon Winwood at the last moment. He had scarcely time to familiarize himself with the routine duties of his office before the session began. He had no time at all to change the programme so that it would suit his own capabilities or be more palatable to the House.

In the second place, Winwood was totally without parliamentary experience. He afterwards said that the first speech that he ever heard in the House of Commons was his own. A comparatively insignificant bureaucrat, he could not be left to work out the details of the programme as Salisbury had done. So a greater burden was thrown on the King, who disliked daily routine and did not possess the tact and forbearance necessary for dealing with the Commons. The appointment of Winwood at this time, when he laboured under such manifest disadvantages, was a remarkable instance of the King's naïve optimism.

Finally, Winwood's character was his greatest weakness. His virtues were honesty, straightforwardness, courage, and resolution. But in spite of them his personality irritated the House of Commons. His vehement, rash, and combative nature soon gained him a reputation for tactlessness and arrogance. The House of Commons, when confronted with his harsh and blunt manner, was goaded into attacks of increasing violence on royal policies. In the end, the situation passed beyond the control of any leader in the House. Winwood could perhaps have been successful as the second-ranking spokesman of the Crown in the lower House. But he needed experience, an opportunity for preparation, and, above all, the guidance of a competent statesman acting as the Crown's spokesman in the House of Commons.

Chapter VII

The Opening of Parliament

WITH the elections over, a programme prepared, and a new secretary appointed, the Court awaited the opening of parliament with a mixture of foreboding and optimism. Although a few courtiers had high hopes for the session, Chamberlain was coldly realistic in his appraisal of the situation. He believed that the King had simply escaped from one predicament into another by summoning parliament. With more opposition than had been expected, he could see that the lack of courage and initiative among the leading officials would lead to disaster. At best, Chamberlain felt that the Court could do no more than hold its own. Gloomy as his predictions were, in a scant three months he would see them fulfilled.[1]

The second parliament of James's reign opened with great pomp on Tuesday, 5 April 1614. At about eleven o'clock the long procession moved from Whitehall to Westminster Abbey. It was an imposing sight despite lowering skies and gusts of rain. The procession was divided into sections separated by groups of ten trumpeters. First came a double file of gentlemen, clerks of various offices, knights, baronets, judges, and other officials, all on horseback. They were followed by the peers in their robes and the bishops in their vestments. After them came the earl marshal, the lord steward, and the lord chamberlain. Next came Prince Charles wearing a long robe of rich cloth and surrounded by a crowd of gentlemen on foot. Near the end of the procession King James

[1] *Letters of Chamberlain,* i. 515–16.

wearing his crown rode on a fine horse. Following him there was only his favourite, the Earl of Somerset, leading a spare horse.

Even during the procession hidden passions of religious controversy flared. When a bishop fell from his horse, he was taunted by a Puritan noble. But the latter in turn was thrown from his horse and broke an arm to the delight of the Roman Catholics, who saw the hand of God in the discomfiture of both.

The influence of Sarmiento, the Spanish ambassador, was all too apparent. Even though he was half an hour late, the King would not start the procession until he arrived. His position was clear enough to the crowd, which greeted his arrival with shouts: 'Here comes the ambassador of Spain! Now the King will come forth!' Sarmiento's privileged position was also obvious from the arrangements made for him to hear the King's opening speech to parliament. Because strangers were excluded, he could not appear publicly in the House of Lords. But a silk curtain with small holes in it was hung over a recess. Sitting behind the curtain, Sarmiento and his guests, the Danish ambassador and the Spanish archduke's ambassador from Flanders, were able to witness the proceedings.[2]

After a service at the Abbey the King and his followers proceeded on foot to the House of Lords in Westminster Palace. Meanwhile the four privy councillors in the House of Commons (Winwood, Caesar, Parry, and Lake) had been waiting for some time in the Court of Requests, which adjoined St. Stephen's Chapel, where

[2] B.M. Harl. MSS. 5176, f. 32; P.R.O. S.P. Spanish 15/40: 56; P.R.O. Spanish transcripts, 12/35 (Sarmiento to Anover, 7/17 Apr. 1614); *Cal. S.P. Venice, 1613–15*, pp. 115–16; *Letters of Chamberlain*, i. 522–4.

the lower House met. The Earl of Nottingham, the lord high steward, arriving about noon, administered the oaths of allegiance and supremacy to the four councillors and to about twenty other members.

This group then divided into three sections, and administered the oaths to the remaining members in groups of ten or twelve. Although 160 members were present, the whole process was completed in about an hour. Then the members sat in the House for another hour awaiting a summons to the Lords. Finally, when a messenger came, they went to the upper House to hear the King's opening speech. But as in 1604 the arrangements were faulty, an ill omen for the session. When the Commons reached the House of Lords, they found the space allotted to them nearly filled with strangers. Most of the members drifted back to St. Stephen's, leaving only a few to hear the King's speech. There the discontented members sat muttering and grumbling until half past four, waiting for the King to finish.[3]

The King delivered his speech from the throne in the House of Lords. Before him sat the peers in their robes, while among the throng which pressed up to the bar were the few members of the lower House who had managed to find room. The King spoke well, but his eloquence was lost upon most of his intended audience, who sat disconsolately in St. Stephen's awaiting the return of their more fortunate fellows.

The King's speech was divided into three main parts. First he spoke of religion under the heading of *bona animi*. Although he declared that the Papists were increasing, he asked for a revision and better enforcement of existing penal laws rather than new legislation. Here

[3] *Commons jn. i. 455.*

James displayed one of those flashes of vision which occasionally revealed his intellectual capacity. He declared that no belief could be destroyed by persecution, and by implication at least he supported general toleration. If Protestantism was the true religion, Popery would fall through its own errors. But otherwise persecution would simply increase the number of Papists. He declared categorically that no religion, true or false, ever gained by persecuting its enemies.

In the second part of his speech the King spoke of the good of the state under the title *bona corporis*, meaning the security of the dynasty. He declared that he had arranged the marriage of his daughter to a Protestant to prevent her conversion to Roman Catholicism. In the case of England and the Palatinate, as with England and Scotland, the greater power would attract the lesser. While the Palatinate might eventually become an appendage of England, England would never be subordinate to the Palatinate. He asked parliament to naturalize the Count Palatine and his descendants, and to declare them eligible for succession to the throne.

In the third part of his speech the King spoke of *bona fortunae*, meaning his financial necessity. He referred in particular to expenses connected with the Palatine marriage and Ireland. He then denied any intention of bargaining with the Commons. He regarded the affection of his subjects as their greatest gift to him. He wanted nothing from them except what they would grant out of love, and he even left the amount to them.

After these three main sections of his speech the King disclaimed any intention of extending his prerogative. He also denied that he had dealt with the undertakers, had interfered with elections, or had even wanted a

packed parliament. The King declared that his proclamations did not have the force of statute law, but
were intended simply as temporary expedients to meet
situations arising while parliament was not in session.
Once parliament met, it could enact the proclamations
into law or invalidate them. He also stated his intention
to summon parliament more frequently in the future.
After these concessions he stated that he would offer his
bills of grace at another meeting. He cautioned parliament not to prefer trivial matters above these important
affairs of state. Although he would welcome a consideration of grievances, the Commons should not beg for them
from everyone in the street. He also denied that he intended to give proclamations the force of law.

The King opposed frequent conferences between the
two Houses. He wanted this session devoted mainly to
finance, while a second session at Michaelmas would consider grievances. He then elaborated on his affection for
parliament, saying that he hoped for a parliament of love.
To avoid misunderstandings he would deal personally
with the two Houses. In the Michaelmas session he would
ask for nothing, so that the entire session could be devoted to reforms.[4]

The King's speech showed Bacon's influence in almost
every line. Bacon even suggested the mirror simile with
which it began. But Bacon's memorandum contained
nothing like the section on religion, which was original
with the King. The whole section on the Count Palatine,
even to the Latin quotations, followed Bacon's model.
The surprising portion was the section on supply, in
which James was less emphatic than Bacon. Indeed, he
intended to follow Bacon's earlier advice to allow the

[4] *H.M.C. Hastings MSS.* iv. 230–4; Bodleian MS. Eng. Hist. c. 286, f. 47.

Commons much latitude on the supply question. While the speech did not emphasize procedure, here it also followed Bacon in what was included. As Bacon had suggested, the King denied any connexion with the undertakers, and expressed his affection for parliament in fulsome terms. The main point, but an essential one, in which the King departed from Bacon's plan was to promise bills of grace at the beginning of the session. The real departure from Bacon's policies, however, came in the King's speech of 9 April.

When the King had finished his speech, the Commons retired to their own House to choose a Speaker. After a long silence, Sir Ralph Winwood screwed up his courage and rose for his maiden speech. Although his speech was well organized, he must have committed it to memory, for he delivered it 'in a kind of an academicall tune'. Nevertheless Winwood showed considerable self-assurance for a man who had never before heard a speech in the Commons. He simply pointed out the importance of the parliament and the need for an able Speaker. Then he named Ranulph Crew as a wise choice. A general shout for Crew followed without the dissenting voices apparent in 1604. In the choice of a Speaker, at least, the House was more united than it had been ten years earlier. Crew's nomination, however, could not have come as a surprise, for Chamberlain had known of it for almost three weeks.

After another silence Crew rose in the traditional manner to protest his unworthiness. He spoke of his infirmities, and reminded the House that he had served only in the parliament of 1597–8, and even then inconspicuously. He concluded by asking them to choose someone else. In reply Sir Julius Caesar, a privy councillor, declared that Crew's modesty commended him to the House. Winwood and Caesar then escorted Crew to the Speaker's chair amid the general applause of the Commons. The Speaker-elect, still protesting his unworthiness, asked leave of the House to request the King to excuse him from this service. Then he announced that he would be presented to the King on Thursday afternoon.

As Crew had requested, the House assembled at one o'clock on Thursday. This time the serjeant was sent to the House of Lords to see that the area reserved for the Commons was kept unoccupied until their arrival.

Shortly afterwards the Commons were summoned to the House of Lords, where Winwood and Lake presented Crew to the King in full parliament. Crew made the customary speech protesting his unworthiness. This oration, however, appears to have been shorter and simpler than the usual ornate effort. Perhaps its simplicity was a result of the delay in choosing a Speaker. Crew may not have had sufficient time to prepare an elaborate oration. The lord chancellor replied that the King wished Crew to act as Speaker, and he commended the Commons on their choice.

Crew then humbly accepted the position, asking the King for the traditional liberties of the Commons without describing them in specific detail. In his answer granting the Speaker's request, the lord chancellor specified the three liberties: freedom of speech, freedom from arrest, and freedom from misrepresentation. He also urged the Commons to act prudently and emphasized their duty to grant supply. When the lord chancellor had concluded, the Commons returned to their own House with the mace borne before the Speaker. After the reading of a bill against false bail and one or two other trivial matters, the Commons adjourned until the next day.

On Friday the lower House plunged headlong into a controversy over the eligibility of Sir Francis Bacon, the attorney-general. The supporters of the Crown must have had some advance notice of the attempt to exclude Bacon, for when the day's business began, Sir George More, the chancellor of the Order of the Garter, moved for a committee to consider all questions of eligibility. But Edward Duncombe, an obscure Bedfordshire squire and an active opponent of the Court in the previous parliament, promptly moved that the attorney-general should be excluded from the House of Commons and sent up to the House of Lords in an advisory capacity like the judges. Under Alford's leadership the Commons promptly asserted their jurisdiction over the question.

A general debate followed, with few voices raised in Bacon's favour. Sir Roger Owen, a particularly hot-headed member of the opposition, made so violent a speech that an unfriendly critic referred to him as the gentleman 'whose braynes flew up and down in his head, as a Bird flyes in the ayre'. Owen even suggested that privy councillors were admitted only by the courtesy of the Commons. Bacon's only defender, Sir John Savile, a member of the Council of the North, simply praised Bacon's ability.[5]

Finally old Sir Jerome Horsey, a veteran of the Russian trade and a minor official, called for the question, and Bacon's fate seemed sealed. But amid the clamour for a vote, the Speaker at last aroused himself to stem the tide. He first asked if anyone else wished to speak, but the officials were so overawed that none responded. He then

[5] B.M. Add. MSS. 34079, ff. 29–30.

suggested a search for precedents, but was told roughly not to divert the question. His manœuvres, however, had given Francis Moore, a legal supporter of the Crown, time to collect his wits. Moore came to Bacon's defence, but he too failed to divert the House or still the clamour for immediate action.

Sir Herbert Croft, an opposition member in 1610, in his turn tried to mollify the aroused Commons. While favouring the exclusion of Bacon, nevertheless he felt that they should have a committee search for precedents in order to justify their action to the King. Other members, even the highly respected opposition lawyer William Hakewill, came to Croft's support. Their combined efforts calmed the House, and a committee was appointed to search for precedents. Significantly this committee included only three important adherents of the Court and no privy councillors at all. In the general debate not a single important official had defended Bacon. In fact, if Croft had not intervened, Bacon would have been excluded at once. So on the first day of real business the initiative was completely in the hands of the opposition.

Although the Court attempted to divert the Commons the next day with a speech from the King and a series of minor concessions, the House refused to abandon the chase. Although the solicitor-general reviewed the royal concessions and introduced two bills of grace when the Commons reassembled on Monday, they promptly returned to the case of the attorney-general. The committee had to admit that it had found no precedents to justify Bacon's exclusion. At this point Winwood finally rose to defend Bacon. He maintained that the same rules of eligibility should apply to the attorney-general, the king's serjeant, and the solicitor-general, who performed the same duties and were distinguished only by their difference in precedence. In spite of his strong case Winwood asked that Bacon should be admitted as a special favour to the King. Then the House should determine the eligibility of future attorneys-general.

Sir Roger Owen, deprived of the support of precedents, now declared that the absence of favourable precedents was enough. However he was willing to compromise by admitting Bacon but excluding the attorney-general in the future. Sir Richard Williamson, a master of requests, tore Owen's argument to shreds. He declared that the burden of proof rested on those opposing Bacon, and ridiculed the illogicality of admitting the king's serjeant and the solicitor-general, but excluding the attorney-general. Finally James Whitelocke, a lawyer of great prestige and a friend of Bacon, supported Owen's position. After some further debate, in which every speaker supported Whitelocke, the House concurred in the same solution. Bacon was to be admitted as a personal favour, but the attorney-general would be ineligible in the future.

So the Crown suffered a serious and perhaps unnecessary defeat at the very beginning of the session. Even though the final compromise originated with the King, he lost for the future the services of a valuable official in the lower House. Also the Crown's prestige suffered because the attorney-general was admitted on such precarious tenure. It was apparent to contemporaries that the King had been forced to compromise because he feared to face a showdown. The dispute had become so acrimonious that concessions were necessary to pacify the House. Those who favoured the Court were apprehensive of the effects of this initial defeat.

The official group had been demoralized by the attack. Although Bacon's eligibility was first challenged on Friday, 8 April, the House reached its decision only on the following Monday. But the leading officials were not prepared for the debate. When Sir Richard Williamson, no prominent Court supporter, delivered a devastating and completely unanswerable attack on Bacon's opponents, the other officials did not follow up his advantage. The official group, perhaps on orders from the King, simply let a strong case go by default. Already the Crown felt compelled to conciliate the Commons at any price.

The day after the first attack on Bacon (Saturday, 9 April) both Houses assembled in the banqueting chamber at Whitehall Palace to hear the King's second speech of the session. In this speech the King largely abandoned Bacon's ideas in favour of Neville's advice. He again emphasized his desire for a parliament of love. As he was willing to satisfy any just grievances, he hoped that parliament would show its affection by paying his debts and granting him revenue. He also repeated his intention of dealing with the Papists and with Ireland.

The King once more declared his abhorrence of bargaining. He would not act like a merchant making a contract, but he would freely grant certain graces to his subjects as a loving prince. In return, parliament had the duty of relieving his necessities, but he would leave the details to them. In the future, although he would need no extraordinary revenue except in time of war, he would summon parliament periodically to hear their grievances.

The King declared once more that he had not dealt with the undertakers. He stated that he had never objected to anyone elected by the people. He went on to say that he would have been a fool to trust undertakers and that whoever doubted the truth of his protestation would be accusing him of falsehood. Every member of either House to whom he had talked had assured him that parliament would supply his financial needs as soon as it understood them.

After exhorting parliament to consider supply and grievances together, the King had the lord chancellor read a list of eleven bills of grace and three other reforms not yet drafted as bills. These concessions represented the proposals of Neville and the undertakers which had been prepared before parliament met. They were, as we have seen in Chapter VI, matters of secondary importance.

In the concluding portion of his speech the King reverted to the question of money. He once more expressed the belief that parliament would relieve his necessities in return for the bills of grace. He concluded his speech with the promise of a broad general pardon at the end of the session as well as the redress of any other grievances, provided his prerogative was not curtailed.[6]

This second speech of the King, a combination of Neville's proposals and his own wheedling half-measures, made a poor impression. Chamberlain, who believed that the King had lost prestige by his attitude, characterized him as having 'descended as yt were to intreatie to be relieved'. Likewise the bills of grace made little impression. Chamberlain declared they were 'of no great moment', and Sir John Holles, a courtier and member of parliament, stated that the concessions, 'being lean and ill larded, rather irk than please our appetites'.[7]

The King's programme failed to stem the attack on

---

[6] H.M.C. Hastings MSS. iv. 239–41.
[7] Letters of Chamberlain, i. 524–6; H.M.C. Portland MSS. ix. 27–28.

the attorney-general. Although Sir Henry Yelverton, the solicitor-general, made a long speech praising the King and reviewing his bills of grace on the following Monday, the House, as we have seen, promptly returned to Bacon's case without debating the royal programme. In due time all the bills of grace were introduced into the House of Commons, but they created little stir, and most of them died in committee. Two of them, however, passed through all stages in the Commons and were sent up to the House of Lords. The upper House completed action on one of these (a bill to prohibit the collection of private debts by the Crown), but the bill never received the royal assent. The other bill, to repeal the King's authority to legislate for Wales by ordinance, never went beyond the first reading in the upper House. The lower House did not even pass the remaining bills of grace. Neville's programme proved completely inadequate to win for the King the support of the House of Commons.

Meanwhile one item in the royal programme had encountered little opposition. In less than a week the House of Lords had passed and sent to the House of Commons a bill to naturalize the Count Palatine, the husband of James's daughter Elizabeth, and to declare her descendants lawful heirs to the throne. Although the Commons added a clarifying amendment, the Lords quickly concurred, and by 15 April the bill had passed through all stages in both Houses.

When the House of Commons met on Tuesday, 12 April, the day after deciding Bacon's eligibility, it was in a stormy mood. First, members from Plymouth and Bristol attacked, as a monopoly, the French company, which had been chartered in 1611. Trade between England and France was confined to members of this company, which was under the control of the London merchants. The Londoners were accused of oppressive practices like imprisoning interlopers and searching private houses, as well as of ruining the trade of the west country.[8] In order to divert attention from London, Robert Middleton, a member for the City and the lord mayor's brother, introduced a bill against impositions. After that, the House grappled with the explosive religious question. Sir Maurice Berkeley, fresh from his triumph over the master of the rolls in Somerset, attacked the ecclesiastical courts. He was followed by Thomas Wentworth (the son of Peter Wentworth, not the future Earl of Strafford), who demanded Puritanical alterations in the service, a reform of the ministry, and drastic measures against the Papists. Then John Hoskyns devoted a long speech replete with references to Hell and the devil to an attack on the ecclesiastical courts.

Winwood chose this inopportune time to propose a grant of supply. In a carefully-prepared speech he set forth in detail the conditions at home and abroad which made the grant necessary. After an appeal for a favourable hearing, he declared that he spoke not for the King alone, but for the public good as a true Englishman. He believed that the maintenance of true religion and the liberties of England demanded a grant of money.

Winwood tried to identify the welfare of the King with the welfare of the subject. He stated that by summoning parliament the King had chosen the right way to reform abuses and relieve his wants. Winwood then touched on various responsibilities facing the Crown, such as the navy, the garrisons in the Low Countries, the

[8] Letter of Thomas Wentworth, 25 Apr. 1614, in Sheffield Central Library, Wentworth Woodhouse Papers, Strafford MSS., vol. 34.

danger of rebellion in Ireland, and Roman Catholic intrigues on the Continent. He also said that the Commons should vote supply in gratitude for the bills of grace. Winwood concluded by asking for an immediate consideration of the question.[9]

Although Winwood's delivery had improved, this unexpected request provoked an unfavourable reaction in the House. There was an immediate suggestion that reforms should come before supply. One member proposed a committee free from official domination to consider the bills of grace and to propose reforms. Nicholas Fuller, an extreme opposition leader, suggested that the House should wait until the bills of grace had been introduced. Then they should measure their generosity by the benefits received.

Even the leading officials did not give Winwood's proposal the support that they owed to official measures. Sir Julius Caesar, the chancellor of the Exchequer, did make a speech in which he maintained that the security of the state was threatened by lack of money. While he gave no details of royal finance, he offered to disclose the Crown's indebtedness to members privately. But in addition to a large committee on supply Caesar suggested a subcommittee to consider the bills of grace at the same time.

Bacon also made a long speech in favour of a grant. He discussed the difficulties which faced the King in his dealings with foreign nations. He also called on the House to show their affection for the King by granting supply, as he had shown his affection for them by offering graces. The King's business and the business of the commonwealth should proceed together. But in spite of

[9] *H.M.C. Downshire MSS.* iv. 366–9.

his eloquence, Bacon must have sensed the Crown's weakness. Instead of supporting Winwood's demand for an immediate decision, he moved for a committee of the whole on supply.

Sir George More, an official of secondary rank, likewise spoke in favour of supply. But he moved that the House should consider graces one day and supply the next. Sir Henry Montague, the king's serjeant, followed More's suggestion. He proposed that the bills of grace should be considered the next morning, and supply in the afternoon.

But other speakers opposed such prompt consideration of the supply question. Some declared that many members had not yet taken their seats in the House. Hoskyns wanted to wait until the members had received Communion, pointing out quaintly that in the primitive church the offering came at the end of the service. But more and more the Commons dwelt on rumours of undertaking. Member after member denounced any attempt of a few persons to speak for the whole House before the King. Others suggested that the Commons could not act in good conscience until they were cleared of these suspicions. The supply question was lost in this welter of confusion. Even Thomas Crew, the Speaker's brother, joined in the opposition to supply. He suggested that supply should be delayed until after the Easter recess so that the House could determine the country's reaction to the bills of grace. Despite the unexpected support of Whitelocke Winwood's proposal failed of adoption, and supply was deferred until the second Monday after Easter.[10]

Thus the Crown suffered a check on the most

[10] *Commons jn.* i. 461–3.

important question before parliament. Even though Winwood's timing was bad (perhaps this was not his fault), he had done his best, and his speech was well received. But once again Winwood was hampered because his colleagues did not support him. In such an important matter, where unity was essential, Caesar and Bacon made their own proposals. Lake and Parry did not speak at all. Almost the only other officials to support Winwood were Sir Henry Montague and Sir George More. Despite Winwood's single-handed effort, the royal programme suffered a severe defeat, at least partly because its natural supporters did not come to its defence.

On Wednesday, 13 April, the Commons decided to receive Communion together on Palm Sunday (17 April) at St. Margaret's Church instead of Westminster Abbey. Probably the connexion between the lower House and St. Margaret's dates from this incident. Although the change was made because the House disliked the High Church service at the abbey, the Puritanism of the Commons should not be over-emphasized.[11]

The lower House spent the rest of the week on election controversies, minor bills, and nebulous attacks on the undertakers. But on Monday, 18 April, the bill against impositions received its second reading. While many members spoke in favour of the bill, few defended impositions. Sir George More pointed out that the Court of Exchequer had declared impositions legal, and Sir Henry Montague feebly defended the King's position. Most of those who attacked impositions were moderate in their tone and reluctant to override a decision of the courts. Whitelocke and Fuller merely maintained that the House should not reverse its 1610 judgement against imposi-

[11] *Letters of Chamberlain*, i. 524–6.

tions, and Christopher Brooke feared that precedent would make impositions lawful unless the Commons took action.

On the other hand, Sir Herbert Croft made a sweeping declaration that impositions made all property insecure, and Sir Dudley Digges boldly stated that the Exchequer judgement in favour of impositions was erroneous. William Hakewill, who had accepted the Court's judgement at first, declared that he had changed his mind after hearing the debate in 1610. Hoskyns, reaching the heart of the issue, proposed that supply should be deferred until the imposition question was settled. Finally the bill was referred to a committee of the whole House on 3 May, after the Easter recess.

On Wednesday, 20 April, Sir George More protested that the House was considering the bills of grace and postponing supply, even though it had decided to take them up together. Promptly and without debate the House ordered that supply should be deferred until 5 May. After a debate attacking the trade monopoly of the Londoners in the French company, the House adjourned until 2 May for the Easter recess.

The first stage of the Addled Parliament ended with the adjournment for Easter. From the Crown's point of view the first two weeks of the session were neither successful nor reassuring. Parliament's single accomplishment was the passage of the Palatine bill. On the other hand, Bacon had been admitted only on sufferance, and the thorny question of impositions had already appeared. The bills of grace had not mollified the Commons, and the attempt to obtain supply had failed. All the while just beneath the surface were rumours of undertaking and traces of Puritanism, which continually appeared in debates on other issues, like ominous prophecies for the future. The young lawyers were especially vehement, as the only way to gain credit in the Commons was to join in the attack. The initiative was passing from the former leaders of the opposition to the younger and more irresponsible elements.[12]

Winwood himself, harassed almost to death by his problems and duties, and hindered by the jealousy of his rivals at Court, was haunted by nightmares of failure and ruin. Even his slightest gesture was misconstrued, and he had to ignore many petty slights in the House. While Winwood might appear indifferent to taunts and rebuffs, he clearly realized his problems. He knew that the King's financial straits would throw the administration into confusion if he received no money from parliament. Those at Court who hoped for a harmonious session must have looked forward to the end of the recess with a chill in their hearts.[13]

[12] *Letters of Chamberlain*, i. 524–6.
[13] Ibid.; P.R.O. S.P. Venice 99/15, f. 227 (no. 275).

Chapter VIII

Undertakers and Impositions

WHEN parliament reassembled on Monday, 2 May, after the Easter recess, the House of Commons plunged immediately into the two most controversial issues of the session: undertakers and impositions. The government probably sensed the temper of the opposition, for it attempted a counterstroke at the very start of business. Bacon introduced four bills of grace with a conciliatory speech emphasizing the King's bounty. The first bill provided that the estates of attainted persons should be liable for their debts; the second provided for the simplification and codification of the penal laws; the third prohibited inquisitorial judicial procedures; and the fourth provided that in cases of defective land titles the burden of proof should rest on the Crown instead of on the defendant.

But these concessions had no effect on the House. As early as 13 April Sir Roger Owen had made a speech saying that many copies of the King's graces had been in circulation before parliament met. On his suggestion a committee had been appointed to draft a message to the King protesting against undertaking and declaring that the House would grant supply because of their love for the King.

Owen now reported to the House from this committee. Although there was general condemnation of undertaking, no evidence of it had been discovered. Owen made up for the lack of evidence by the violence of his report, in which he declared that the undertakers were more dangerous to parliament than the Gunpowder Plotters. He even denounced anyone except the Speaker who discussed the business of parliament with the King. Ignoring the realities of the electoral system, Owen condemned any member who owed his seat to a peer. The committee asked for additional authority to investigate the whole question of undertaking.

Other members followed Owen in his attack on the undertakers. Nicholas Fuller, an opposition lawyer and a Puritan, supported a further investigation because he had heard 'that some One great Man [probably the Earl of Northampton], had, by Letters, procured Sixty Voices' in the House of Commons. John Hoskyns likewise demanded a fuller investigation, blaming the whole affair on the Papists and comparing it to the Trojan horse. Hoskyns's speech caused Sir Dudley Digges to admit that he had circulated the report about the Papists. But the report had spread so far and so fast that Digges now feared it was all 'some false Rumour, spread to hinder the great Businesses now in hand' in parliament.[1]

But the debate was not at all one-sided. Sir Henry Poole, a Wiltshire squire, criticized members for wasting time on vague rumours unsupported by evidence. Others supported his stand and called on the House to heal the wound rather than irritate it, because one baseless accusation would simply give rise to others. As no undertakers had been discovered, a simple protestation would clear the House, and they could go on with the business of the kingdom.

Sir Francis Bacon then delivered a long and eloquent speech in an attempt to settle the question. He scoffed at the whole concept because the members of the House did not make up their minds until they had heard the

[1] *Commons jn.* 1. 471.

debates. He pointed out that no individual had been accused of undertaking and that the King had twice denied having any part in it. But the question should be settled because otherwise a cloud of suspicion would rest on the whole House. No one could defend royal policies without being suspected of undertaking, and the people would be uneasy if they thought that parliament had betrayed them.

Bacon then differentiated between proper and improper advice to the King about parliament. He declared that it was quite proper to advise the King to summon parliament and even to suggest concessions. But it was improper to attempt to drive the Commons like sheep, or to spread rumours of undertaking and packing. He opposed an investigation of undertaking because he could not see where it should begin. He ended with the suggestion that the Commons should send a message to the King denying that they were tainted with undertaking.[2]

But all Bacon's eloquence failed to sway the House. In the end they decided that a committee of the whole should investigate undertaking on Wednesday afternoon. The King, however, made an attempt to forestall them. He summoned the Commons hastily before him on Wednesday afternoon, deferring the committee until Thursday. In his third speech to the lower House James declared that his right to levy impositions rested on a judgement of the Court of Exchequer Chamber. Although he would not permit any infringement on his prerogative, he would allow the case to be reheard.

The King expressed the hope that he would not have to ask parliament for financial relief again. He declared that he would not bargain with them, but would depend on

---

[2] Spedding, *Letters and Life of Bacon*, v. 42–48.

their love. He also denied once more that he had dealt with the undertakers. The King maintained that his declaration would clear the Commons of undertaking without further debate.[3]

But the King's speech had no effect on the Commons. Although Sir George More reminded the House the next day that they had planned to consider supply on that date, they promptly decided to hear the report from the committee on impositions first. Sir Edwin Sandys, who delivered the report, made a long speech citing the usual medieval precedents. Sandys proposed a petition to the King instead of a bill because the Lords could stifle a bill. His motion that supply should be deferred until the impositions question had been settled won general approval.

But there was no unanimity about anything except a general criticism of impositions. Some members, fearing the opposition of the Lords, wanted a petition to the King. Others, who remembered that a similar petition in 1610 had yielded no results, wanted a bill, suggesting that they should 'tender this tenderly to the Lords, with special Recommendation to them' for its passage. Still others wanted both a petition and a bill. As the debate proceeded, the House became more and more excited until members were shouting each other down in the midst of a general uproar. One veteran member who attempted to shame the House into order by comparing it to a cockpit was himself denounced for 'assuming too much Regularity to himself'. Moderate opposition leaders like James Whitelocke advised the House to continue with supply while they considered impositions, but less experienced members spoke of postponing subsidies, and brought up the undertakers again.

[3] *Commons Debates 1621*, vii. 631–3.

When Leonard Bawtrey, a legal supporter of the Crown, tried to defend the King's stand on impositions, he met with a hostile reception. When he declared that the King had the power to decide when supply should be considered, he was hissed down by the House.

Sir Edwin Sandys and other members then condemned a suggestion for a conference with the Lords on impositions in the King's presence. They feared that the King would overawe the Commons as he had done on previous occasions. The House finally adopted Sandys's motion for a conference with the Lords on impositions.[4]

A new attempt was now made to obtain a grant of supply. Robert Middleton, who had introduced the bill against impositions, was so disturbed by the storm he had raised that he suggested a compromise. He proposed that a subsidy should be collected while the impositions question was being settled, so that an immediate cash grant could be made to the King as soon as an agreement had been reached. When this proposal fell flat, Sir Thomas Lake, a privy councillor, moved for a vote on supply at once. But various other members opposed him, predicting a defeat for the Crown and dissatisfaction in the country.

Sir Edwin Sandys now entered the debate on supply. Although he favoured a grant, he believed that there was no emergency demanding its passage so early in the session. Sandys proposed a message to the King stating that the Commons intended to vote supply unanimously at the proper time. Although Winwood asked the House to set a definite date for supply, they finally decided to inform the King they would grant subsidies unanimously near the end of the session.

<hr/>

[4] *Commons jn.* i. 472-4; *Commons Debates 1621*, vii. 633-4.

On Monday, 9 May, the House of Commons took up the Stockbridge election case. Sir Thomas Parry, the chancellor of the Duchy and a privy councillor, was accused of unlawful interference in the Stockbridge election, the details of which have already been given in Chapter III. The lower House, which believed that it had finally discovered one of the elusive undertakers, suspended Parry from his seat and refused him a hearing while the case was investigated.

The next day the Commons returned to the Stockbridge case with relish. Parry's own threatening letters were produced, and the poverty-stricken voters whom he had coerced testified against him. Supporters of the Crown could find little to say in Parry's defence. William Fanshawe, the auditor of the Duchy, actually did Parry more harm than good in an attempt to defend him. Sir George More cited Parry's age and long public career, and tried to shift the blame to his subordinates. Sir Robert Phelips suggested that Parry should be suspended temporarily and then pardoned. Bacon cited Parry's age and service, and asked the House to be generous because they did not live in an ideal commonwealth. He maintained that the chancellor of the Duchy had the prescriptive right to nominate one member from each Duchy town, and suggested legislation to reform electoral abuses. Sir Henry Montague and Edward Mosley, the attorney-general of the Duchy, also defended Parry.

But the official group was unable to save Parry. Some members believed that the punishment of so great an official would be a salutary lesson. Others accused him of undertaking. Still others even demanded the abolition of the Duchy's separate chancery court.

Although Lake did little for Parry, Winwood finally

came to his defence. But he too was forced to admit the seriousness of the charge. He simply declared the King's intention to punish Parry unless the Commons interceded for him. As usual the King's message only irritated the House, and several members protested that his interference violated their liberties. Finally the House ordered Winwood to thank the King, but to tell him that they wished to deal with Parry themselves.

The next morning, when Parry's case came up again, Winwood informed the House that the King would suspend Parry from the council. Without further debate Parry was expelled from the House. Although some prominent opposition leaders including Edward Alford, Sir James Perrot, and Sir Edwin Sandys, wished to extend mercy to Parry, the House concluded the case by sending a message to the King saying that they were doubly satisfied with their own censure and with the King's punishment of Parry.[5]

Thus Sir Thomas Parry fell into disgrace with little attempt on the part of the Crown (futile though it might have proved) to defend him. To some extent Parry was betrayed by his associates. William Fanshawe, the auditor of the Duchy, discredited Parry more under pretence of defending him than those who attacked him most bitterly. Apart from his message offering to punish Parry, the King took no part in the case. Perhaps Parry had become so useless with advancing years (he was over sixty) that James welcomed this opportunity to get rid of him. Also Parry's conduct was almost indefensible. Even so well-disposed a commentator as Lorkin had to admit that the accusation was true.[6]

[5] *Commons Debates 1621*, vii. 637; *H.M.C. Portland MSS.* ix. 132.
[6] *Court and Times of James I*, i. 314–18.

This event, relegated by Gardiner to a footnote, must have shaken the prestige of the council to its foundations. For a type of electioneering which was not uncommon in that period one of the King's close advisers had been expelled from the lower House. Not only had the Commons deprived him of his seat, but also their action had led to his suspension from the council table. Any privileged position in the House which had protected the councillors from attack now disappeared completely. This development would force them to act with care lest they lay themselves open to attack by the hostile Commons. Hence their sphere of activity narrowed, and they felt more acutely the dilemma of serving two masters. While the House would mistrust them as tale-bearers to the King, the King would demand services of the councillors which would bring the wrath of the House down upon them. Finally, Parry's condemnation was certain to lower the prestige of the councillors elected to the lower House. Now that the Commons had proved a councillor to have feet of clay, all the councillors were reduced to the level of ordinary mortals, and could be dealt with accordingly. On the other hand, the commoners who sat at the council-table lost prestige in the eyes of the peers on the council. If they had so little influence in the Commons that they could not protect themselves, their opinions were valueless, and their usefulness was limited to service as clerks or messenger-boys. Once the Commons had forced the King to dismiss a councillor even for a heinous offence, the development had begun which led ultimately to parliamentary control of the executive.

Meanwhile the committee on undertakers under the chairmanship of Sir Roger Owen was trying to separate fact from rumour with little success. During the debate on supply on 5 May, Francis Ashley, a lawyer, had said that before parliament met he had been given the schedule of business for the first four or five days of the session. In the committee on undertakers the same afternoon he was pressed for further details.

Mr. Ashlye sayed in the morninge that matters were Come ripe of examination, but was loathe to name particulars till, beinge beged by the whole house he saide at his Comminge first to towne he was saluted with bills of grace that are nowe presented from the king, and with more it was farther alledged that noble men engrossed the burgesshippes, some 8, some 10. The effect of Mr. Ashlyes speache was, that Sir Reynolde Moore [Sir Robert More, a courtier?] told him of a merchant that said there were undertakers, he denied it but it was approved to his face by Sir Jhon Crompten, besides. Prince Henry did expostulate with Sir Thomas Overburye wherefore he was so greate with some men who aunswered that they were to doe the kinge good service in the next parliament. Layinge the report uppon Sir Jhon Sams and he uppon Mr. Briton and Mr. Briton on Mr. Gibbs, but nothinge was gathered therbye and so an end to that.[7]

Still the committee continued its search for under-takers. When it met a week later, the members almost came to blows. Late in the afternoon, when most of the committee-members had already left, a paper listing concessions for parliament was produced and attributed to the undertakers. Two royalist members, Sir William Herbert and Sir Robert Killigrew, who were about to leave, assailed the chairman, Sir Roger Owen, charging him with bias. They accused him of plotting to produce the paper only after they had left. When he pleaded that

[7] *Commons Debates 1621*, vii. 634.

he had forgotten about it, they scoffed at his excuse. Then one of them seized the chair, and the other tried to drag him out of it, crying that 'they would see him forth ere they went, lest he did put tricks upon them'. It is significant that Herbert was the cousin and dependent of the Earl of Pembroke, Neville's chief backer in the privy council. With the example of the tumultuous Irish parliament fresh in their minds, the Commons decided to deal severely with the two offenders. They were both compelled to withdraw from the House and were readmitted only after they had apologized for their conduct.[8]

The final debate on undertaking came on 14 May when Owen gave the last report from his committee. He now exhibited to the House the list of concessions which had been produced in committee. When the paper was read, Sir Henry Neville admitted that it was the one which he had presented to the King at Windsor in July of 1612. He justified his whole programme by disclaiming any attempt to manage parliament. He was able to convince the Commons that his intent was to improve relations between the King and parliament. In the end they decided that he had not done anything unworthy of a good subject and an honest man.[9]

Thus the whole tumult over undertakers, which had unsettled the Commons for weeks, was allowed to fade into obscurity. Neither the Commons nor any later investigator has discovered evidence of a widespread conspiracy to undermine the independence of parliament. Indeed, several well-informed sources, including the Spanish and Venetian correspondence, make no reference

[8] *H.M.C. Portland MSS.* ix. 132–3.
[9] Ibid.; *Commons Debates 1621*, vii. 639–40; *Court and Times of James I*, i. 314–18; *Letters of Chamberlain*, i. 530–1.

to undertaking at all. The rumours about undertakers were based on an exaggerated report of Neville's proposed programme of concessions and the electioneering activities of privy councillors, as well as others, detailed in Chapter III. Neville's programme, as we have seen, was too trifling to attract support. Official electioneering, while probably greater than in 1604, was no more than the normal Elizabethan practice.

Although nothing more than this lay behind the rumours, still undertaking had an unfortunate effect on parliament. To begin with, it wasted time. Day after day the Commons had pursued will-o'-the-wisps, each member feeling impelled to add his bit to the debate. Day after day really important matters were postponed. Nerves wore thin because no progress was made in solving the problems facing parliament. In the second place, the very nebulous character of the whole matter bred suspicion of all who supported the Crown, and especially of the leading officials. Parry's expulsion, of course, served to increase this feeling of mistrust. This aura of suspicion undermined the leadership of the officials and paved the way for a complete break between the King and the Commons. Thirdly, the passions of the House were inflamed by violent speeches on undertaking. With many young and inexperienced members and with only untried officials to guide them, the House tended more and more to get beyond control. Even the seasoned leaders of the opposition lost their influence in the end, and the Commons became more an unruly mob than a legislative assembly. Finally, the officials fell between two stools when they attempted to regain their lost prestige by supporting popular measures. Neither side regarded them as sincere or trustworthy. They alienated important elements at Court without securing the firm support of the Commons.

The most surprising aspect of undertaking is the impact which it had on the Commons. Although its basis in fact was simple and easily explained, it kept the House from advancing public business for weeks on end. So well was this objective achieved that it gives rise to speculation about its cause. The one element in England that had resolutely opposed a parliament was the Spanish faction, dominated by the Howard family. Their reason was simple: without money James was helpless and could not interfere with Spanish designs on the Continent. If parliament met, it would provide him with money, and it would serve as a forum to inflame public opinion against Spain.

As long as they could, the Spanish faction prevented the summoning of a parliament. But early in 1614, to the surprise of their opponents on the privy council, they threw their support to the other side. At the same time the Earl of Suffolk (Thomas Howard) formed an unnatural and insincere alliance with the leader of the Protestant faction, the Earl of Pembroke, in support of Neville and the undertakers. The Howards, too, were active in securing seats in parliament for supporters and even opponents. Sir Edwin Sandys owed his seat to the treasurer of the navy, a dependent of the Earl of Nottingham (Charles Howard). John Hoskyns, who was ardent in pursuit of the undertakers, was linked indirectly with the Earl of Northampton (Henry Howard) before the Addled Parliament ended. It is significant too that Neville's proposed concessions were circulated widely among members of the House of Commons before parliament met. Sir William Herbert's attempt to suppress this information hints that the concessions were circulated without the approval of the Earl of Pembroke.

Probably when the Spanish faction found that it could no longer postpone parliament, it adopted the next best policy: to ensure that the parliament would be a failure. The Howards were shrewd enough to realize that rumours of undertaking, properly stimulated, might achieve the desired objective, especially if hot-headed leaders were assured seats in parliament. Consequently Suffolk joined with Pembroke in support of Neville. He also took care that copies of Neville's proposals, as well as vague reports of electioneering, should float around London before parliament met. The rumours growing out of these activities could easily be exaggerated out of all proportion to the detriment of a harmonious parliament. Whatever part the Howards may have had in undertaking, by 14 May, when the question was finally laid to rest, an almost irreparable breach between King and parliament had been created.

Sensing the temperament of the House, Winwood and Lake decided that they could best restore their waning prestige by advocating reforms in the Established Church. On Friday, 6 May, just after the attack on impositions, Winwood moved that a committee on recusants should meet the next Monday afternoon. In this committee he attacked the clergy for their neglect of preaching and catechizing. He condemned non-residence, pluralities, and the low moral tone of the clergy. Winwood also accused Henry Spiller, the official who received the fines paid by recusants, of misappropriating the money. On 12 May, the day after Parry's expulsion, a bill against non-residence and pluralities had its second reading. Sir Thomas Lake, who owed his position on the council to the Howards, supported the bill and attacked the bishops.[10]

While these manœuvres did assist Winwood in the House, they brought the whole of the clergy down on his back. The mildest epithet that they hurled at him was Puritan, and he was even accused of being a Brownist. The clergy tried to convince the King that Winwood wanted to become the leader of the Puritans, and they assailed him bitterly in the pulpit and in convocation. But Winwood, who remained in the King's good graces, was able to withstand them. Still, between parliament in the morning, committee-meetings in the afternoon, and the other duties of an office in which he was not yet thoroughly settled, Winwood found himself so overwhelmed with business that he scarcely had time for even the sketchiest planning of his parliamentary strategy.[11]

Meanwhile the House had gone back to impositions, with Sir Edwin Sandys reporting from committee on 12 May. He declared that impositions affected the whole kingdom indirectly even though their direct effects fell only on the merchants. The committee recommended that the Commons should confer with the Lords on the subject because impositions not authorized by parliament were illegal. Most of the report dealt with the statement which the Commons would make at this conference and with the persons who would present each section. As there were some objections to details in the report, it was recommitted for revision.[12]

On 16 May the conference came up once more in the House, and the Commons agreed to postpone it until

---

[10] *Commons Debates 1621*, vii. 636, 639.
[11] *Letters of Chamberlain*, i. 528–31.
[12] *Commons Debates 1621*, vii. 638–9.

everyone was prepared. Some of the leading officials, especially Sir Henry Montague and Sir Francis Bacon, were assigned important roles in the conference. Some few members of the House were still unconvinced of the illegality of impositions. But when the House questioned the officials, Bacon, Montague, and Solicitor-General Yelverton denied that there were any records which proved the legality of the King's stand. In this debate and in a succeeding one on the same subject, a few members, especially Leonard Bawtrey, a lawyer, and Thomas Hitchcock, who owed his seat to the Earl of Northampton, supported the legality of impositions.[13]

On 19 May the Commons finally agreed on their statement to the Lords on impositions, but Winwood, who was sent to the upper House to ask for a conference, found that the Lords had already risen. The next time that the Lords met, on Saturday, 21 May, they sent word that they would reply to the Commons' request on Monday. The Lords' debate on this question was to precipitate a new crisis.

Contemporaries were aware of the significance of the three weeks that had elapsed since parliament returned from the Easter recess. For example, Lorkin believed that the officials had blundered when they did not force a vote on the supply question on 5 May. He felt that once Sandys, Digges, and the other opposition leaders had drawn the House away to impositions, the strength of the Court faction was bound to wane rapidly. Puysieux, the French envoy, saw the close connexion between supply and impositions. Although he realized how distasteful any restrictions would be to the King, he believed that James would have to compromise in the end if he

[13] Ibid. 640–2.

wanted to obtain supply. According to Puysieux the Crown could not be sure of support even in the House of Lords. More discerning (or perhaps more frank) than Lorkin, he predicted that the King would dissolve this parliament in a fit of anger as he had the last one.[14]

Those who had opposed a session of parliament saw their dire predictions materialize in the three weeks after Easter. The Commons had been led into greater and greater violence by the rumours of undertaking. More and more the House took on the character of a cockpit, when members delivered more extreme attacks on the Court than they may have intended under the influence of the supercharged atmosphere. The main purpose of the session (from the Crown's point of view) had been forced into the background. Despite Winwood's forcefulness and Bacon's cajolery, the House refused to vote on subsidies, and as the days passed, the hope of an eventual grant waned.

The programme put forward by Neville and his associates to conciliate the Commons had failed completely. Although the Commons regarded the concessions offered by the Crown as trivial, nevertheless these concessions suggested to them that they should demand reforms before voting subsidies. At this point impositions became the central issue. Both sides seemed to have an instinctive understanding of their importance. The real issue at stake was the question of sovereignty, and the King was quite right when he maintained that he would diminish his prerogative seriously if he conceded this point. On the other hand, the Commons were doomed to be junior

---

[14] *Court and Times of James I*, i. 314–18; P.R.O. French transcripts, 3/47 (Puysieux to Buisseaux 11/21 May 1614); P.R.O. French transcripts, 3/48 (Puysieux to Buisseaux 22 May/1 June 1614).

partners, or perhaps no partners at all, in the government if they did not succeed. As the astute French envoy informed his superiors, the atmosphere at Westminster was so tense that only a spark was needed for an explosion.

Chapter IX

Noli Me Tangere

ONLY a few days after Puysieux's dispatch the explosion which he had predicted destroyed all hope of a harmonious session. On Saturday afternoon, 21 May, while the Commons were waiting for the Lords to answer their request for a conference, they debated impositions once more. For the first time leading courtiers attempted an uncompromising defence of the King's position.

The first speaker was Sir Henry Wotton, whose long service as ambassador to Venice had given him a wide knowledge of continental affairs. He declared that precedents did not clearly deny the King's power to impose. Then he divided kings into two classes: elective and hereditary. Elective kings could not impose, because they received their thrones by the will of the people and were dependent on them. But hereditary kings had greater powers because they inherited their crowns. Wotton then cited examples to support his arguments. The Emperor and the King of Poland, both of whom were elected, levied impositions only with the consent of their diets. But every petty Italian prince levied impositions on his own authority. In Spain the King could impose in Castile, where he was an hereditary monarch, but not in Aragon, where he was elected. The King of France not only levied impositions, but he forced the people to buy salt, on which there was an internal levy. The implication of Wotton's argument was of course that James, as a hereditary king, had the right to levy impositions.

Winwood supported Wotton's contentions. He maintained that foreign princes did not impose by law, but by their royal prerogative. He cited the princes of Germany and Italy and the King of Spain as princes using their prerogative powers to impose. He also denied the opposition's contention that the French estates had consented to the levy of impositions.

Most of the leading opponents of the Court replied to Wotton and Winwood. Sir Roger Owen declared that the kings of Spain and France violated their own laws by levying impositions. He referred to history as proof that the French kings gained the power to impose by seldom summoning their estates. Owen also stated boldly that all kings had originally received their crowns by election and with the consent of their subjects. But he made a more telling point when he said that in the last analysis not history, but the ancient laws of England should determine the question. Sir Thomas Roe attacked the arguments of Wotton and Winwood, while Sir Dudley Digges expanded Owen's final point that the King's powers rested on English law, not on continental practice.

Sir Edwin Sandys developed Owen's contract theory in a long and bitter speech. He maintained that the power to impose had led to tyranny in France. At first all kings were elected, and there were reciprocal conditions between the king and his people. Sandys even hinted at the right of revolution. He also denied that the King of England had the right to impose simply because the French king levied impositions.

The boldest speech of all was delivered by Thomas Wentworth, the Puritan son of Peter Wentworth. With typical Puritan zeal Wentworth maintained that impositions were sinful, calling down Divine wrath on those who levied them. For this sin the Spaniards had been punished by the loss of the Low Countries, and Henry IV of France had died like a calf under the butcher's knife. Wentworth cited various texts from the Revelation and Ezekiel, but especially Daniel xi. 20: 'Then shall stande up in his place in the glorie of the kingdome, one that shall rayse taxes: but after fewe dayes hee shall bee destroyed, neither in wrath, nor in battell. And in his place shal stand up a vile person, to whome they shall not give the honour of the kingdome: but hee shall come in peaceably, and obteine the kingdome by flatteries.' A report of this speech, which practically ended the debate, soon reached the ears of the King.[1]

Meanwhile the Lords had been debating the request of the Commons for a conference on impositions. When the Lords received the message from the lower House on Saturday, 21 May, they replied that they would send an answer as soon as it was convenient and began to debate the question. The first speaker was Bishop Neile of Lincoln—like most of the bishops a man of humble origin. The son of a tallow-chandler, he had enjoyed from his youth the patronage of the Cecils, through whose efforts he received a university education, became Dean of Westminster, and in 1608 was made Bishop of Rochester. By early 1614 he had become Bishop of Lincoln. Neile enjoyed the favour of both James I and Charles I, and eventually (in 1631) became Archbishop of York, a position that he held until his death in 1640. An early friend and patron of Laud, Neile was strongly anti-Puritan. Although he had no great intellectual powers, he pos-

---

[1] *Commons Debates 1621*, vii. 644; *Letters of Chamberlain*, i. 532–5; P.R.O. French transcripts 3/48 (Puysieux to Buisseaux 30 May/8 June 1614). The Biblical quotation is from the Geneva version, probably the one with which Wentworth was familiar.

sessed great capacity for business and was popular both at Court and among his clergy. While his best quality was common sense, his greatest defect was lack of foresight. Often, as now in 1614, he failed to realize the consequences of his own rash actions.

Neile's opening speech in this debate was a strongly worded attack on those who did not accept impositions as part of the royal prerogative. He implied that the Commons were disloyal to debate the question at all.

My Lords, I thinke it a daungerous thinge for us to conferre with them aboute the pointe of impositions. For it is a *Noli me tangere*, and none that have ether taken the Othe of Supremecy or Alegence may doe it with a good conscience, for in the Othe of Alegence we are sworne to maintayne the privilidges of the Crowne, and in this conference we should not conferre about a flower, but strike at the roote of the Imperiall Crowne, and therefore in my opinion it is neather fitte to conferre with them nor give them a meetinge.[2]

For greater freedom of debate the Lords then adjourned themselves into a committee of the whole. The lord chancellor brought up what eventually became the crucial point at issue in the upper House. He suggested that the Lords should consult the judges on the legality of impositions before they answered the Commons. The Earl of Southampton, the leading opposition peer, suggested a meeting with the Commons instead of a conference. At a meeting the Lords would listen to the arguments of the Commons, but would not debate the issue with them. This proposal met with general agreement, and it was adopted by the committee of the whole. When the upper House met on Monday, 71 lords were

[2] *H.M.C. Hastings MSS.* iv. 249.

present, of whom 55 were lay peers and 16 were bishops. As Saturday's debate on the conference had been in a committee of the whole, the question came up again on Monday. Although Lord St. John, an opposition peer, contended that the Lords had decided on a meeting on Saturday and asked them to set the time and place, he was opposed by the privy councillors in the upper House. The lord chancellor once more suggested a consultation with the judges. He was supported by the Earls of Suffolk, Nottingham, Pembroke, and Worcester, as well as by Nottingham's heir, Lord Howard de Walden. Two other privy councillors, Lord Knollys and Lord Zouch, also supported the lord chancellor. Among the lords spiritual, Archbishop Abbot of Canterbury and Bishop Montague of Bath and Wells, the brother of the king's serjeant, both spoke in support of the lord chancellor.

Bishop Neile now delivered a second speech on the question, strongly in favour of consulting the judges before any decision was reached. He again accused the Commons of sedition.

My Lords: To what purpose will it be to meete with the lower house? For I am against both the meeteinge and conference. If we should conferre we are not provided, and to meete what good will that doe but to gase one upon an other? Therefore I humbly pray your Lordships that you would heare the Judges touchinge the Kinges right, and not to suffer him to be beaten untill we heare them speake whoe are the fittest to give us light, and untill we heare them lett us not condemne the matter. I doubt if we should meete with the lower house there would passe from them undewtyfull and seditious speches unfitte for us to heare.[3]

[3] *H.M.C. Hastings MSS.* iv. 253.

Several opposition peers attacked the privy councillors' position. The Earl of Southampton maintained that they were debating whether or not to meet the Commons, and that the opinion of the judges on this point was unnecessary. He was supported by the Earl of Dorset, Lord de la Warr, and other peers. Lord Spencer criticized Bishop Neile for accusing the Commons before they had been heard. At the conclusion of the debate the lord chancellor reiterated his contention that the judges should be consulted.

The Lords then voted on the question of consulting the judges before they decided about meeting the Commons. Those favouring a consultation won 39 to 30. The Earl of Pembroke, a privy councillor, and the Earl of Southampton, who acted as tellers, accounted for the two missing votes. The backbone of the majority was made up of bishops and privy councillors. All of the 16 spiritual lords present except the Archbishop of York supported the Crown. Ten lay privy councillors should be added to the bishops, all the councillors present except Pembroke, who acted as a teller. The two Scotsmen in the House of Lords (Richmond and Somerset) are included among the councillors. Of the remaining 43 lay lords, only 14 voted with the Court, while 29 were in opposition.[4]

The narrow margin of the Court's victory was striking. Of the 55 lay peers present, including privy councillors, only 25 supported the King's position while 30 voted against him. The 14 lay lords outside the council who supported the Court probably included several who were under obligation to the Crown or were close relatives of councillors, such as the Earl of Montgomery, Viscount

[4] Ibid. 249–55; *Letters of Chamberlain*, i. 532–5; B.M. Lansd. MSS. 513, ff. 143–52.

Lisle, Lord Danvers, Lord Howard de Walden, and Lord Howard of Effingham. Even in 1614 only about a quarter of the independent lay peers would support the Crown on so vital an issue as impositions.

After this decision six of the judges retired to the lord chancellor's lodgings and spent half an hour in conference. At the end of this time the judges returned and gave their answer through Lord Chief Justice Coke, whose principles dominated their reply. He declared that the judges were sworn to deliver opinions on judicial questions between party and party, and between King and subject. On one side the subject claimed as his birthright freedom from impositions levied by the King's absolute power. But the King maintained that his power to impose was a sovereign right of his prerogative. If it was part of his prerogative, it was warranted by law, for the King had only those prerogatives given him by law. Coke went on to state that the judges were not called before the Lords to dispute, but to advise. A case should be argued by the King's learned counsel, who should by rights attend the House of Lords. The judges would deliver their opinion after the Lords and Commons had argued the case, but not before. Coke concluded by condemning both those who would restrict the prerogative to gain popularity, and those who would extend it beyond its lawful limits to gain favour at Court.[5]

This somewhat anticlimactic result of the debate typified Coke's theory of the position of the judges. He believed that they should be non-political umpires between King and Commons, deciding great questions of state on the principles of the common law. They would hold themselves aloof from the wrangling of everyday

[5] *H.M.C. Hastings MSS.* iv. 256–7; B.M. Lansd. MSS. 513, ff. 143–52.

debate, and would be immune from royal or popular pressure. But this exalted ideal of the judicial function fell to the ground when Coke's dismissal opened the way for the King to influence the decisions of the judges. It could never have become a reality, however, when the two contending parties did not share Coke's veneration for the common law and its interpreters.

The next day (Tuesday, 24 May) the Lords considered whether or not to have a meeting with the Commons on impositions. Once more the opposition peers favoured a meeting, and the privy councillors opposed it. The Earl of Southampton made the principal speech in favour of the proposal. His chief reason was that a refusal would irritate the Commons and injure the King. He also condemned those who accused the Commons of sedition, an obvious slap at Neile. Lord Chandos maintained that they did not need to ask the King's permission to debate impositions. Lord Rich, Lord Spencer, and Lord North supported Southampton without adding any new arguments to his case.

The privy councillors were the most prominent speakers on the other side. Lord Knollys contended that the abolition of impositions would harm the King without benefiting the subject. The merchants would simply charge the same prices and pocket the difference. The Earl of Nottingham maintained that impositions should not be questioned without the King's consent. The lord chancellor asserted that a meeting would accomplish nothing. In a conference the Lords would be at a hopeless disadvantage because they had no legal counsel. As all prerogative powers rested on law, he suggested that impositions should come before the Lords in their judicial capacity on writ of error in a test case. Three other privy councillors, the Earls of Pembroke and Suffolk, and Lord Zouch, also opposed the meeting.

Several spiritual lords spoke in support of the privy councillors. They included Archbishop Abbot of Canterbury, Bishop Parry of St. Asaph, Bishop Montague of Bath and Wells, Bishop Bilson of Winchester, and Bishop James of Durham. For the third time Bishop Neile of Lincoln took a strong stand against the Commons.

My Lords: I beseech yow to give me leave to use a word or two about the pointe of impositions. For that his Majestie hath soe declared himselfe in his speech to the lower house at his last meeteinge with them and seinge the Judges are not fitte to dispute but to judge the case. If any man be agreeved about the pointe of impositions lett him bringe his writte of error, and then the matter may be tried. Otherwise for my part I hould it not fitte that wee (nay but doe decline it) do dispute *de iure Regis aut colore*, and for these reasons I cannot give my consent ether to conferre, or so much as to meete with them about this buissines.[6]

The lord chancellor concluded the debate by delivering a message from the King. The King thanked the Lords for their affection towards him and expressed the desire that they would not make any decisions affecting his prerogative without first consulting the learned counsel and the judges. The Lords then decided without a division not to have a meeting with the Commons on impositions at this time. They sent a message to this effect to the Commons on Thursday, 26 May. Contemporaries sensed that the Lords' decision would irritate the Commons, and this belief was shared by the lord chancellor,

[6] *H.M.C. Hastings MSS.* iv. 259.

who took care to draw up a lengthy memorandum justifying the stand of the upper House.[7]

Meanwhile reports of Neile's attacks on the Commons were spreading through London, and on Wednesday, 25 May, the House first took official notice of his speeches. Although it was probably Sir Mervyn Audley, the youthful son and heir of Lord Audley, who brought the matter to the attention of the Commons, it appears that Sir Robert Phelips, the son of the master of the rolls, first accused Neile by name. Although the Commons had no basis for the report but rumour, young Phelips wanted to send a message to the Lords asking if the report were true. His speech also contained a threat to break off relations with the upper House if they ignored the Commons' request.

Meanwhile Thomas Wentworth had been struck with dismay at the prospect of what he had said on Saturday. He now explained that in his attack on impositions his reference to the assassination of Henry IV of France was not meant to reflect on their own king. As James had found precedents for impositions and had levied them on the advice of his privy council, he should be excused of all blame even if they were illegal. It was moved that Wentworth should be cleared of any seditious intent, 'Which done by a general Acclamation'.[8]

Once Wentworth had made his peace (or so he thought), other members followed Phelips in attacking Neile. Punning on his surname, they accused him of trying to act as high and mighty as the great O'Neill, Earl of Tyrone. Sir William Strode, a courtier, first suggested a suspension of all business until the Commons

[7] Ibid. 257–64; B.M. Cott. MSS. Titus F iv, ff. 257–8.
[8] *Commons jn.* i. 496.

had been cleared of sedition in the eyes of the King. John Hoskyns seized the opportunity to attack the whole episcopal system. He accused Neile of plundering his diocese and suggested that its revenues should be turned over to the King for seven years. Another member believed Neile was 'Worthy to have his Head set on Tower-hill'.[9] A third accused him of sedition. Sir Roger Owen attacked the clergy as a whole in a bitter speech. He declared that Neile's attack was a greater treason than the murder of a judge, and he accused the clergy of supporting absolutism. Owen went so far as to maintain that the Spanish Cortes had more liberty than the English parliament. He concluded by demanding that the House of Lords should send Neile to the Commons for punishment.

The more sensible leaders of the opposition were alarmed by the violence of the lower House, especially because their information about Neile's speeches was based solely on rumour. Sir Dudley Digges warned them to proceed cautiously until they had proof of Neile's remarks. Edward Alford suggested the Commons' favourite device, a search for precedents. Christopher Brooke opposed a suspension of business because it would punish the King and the Commons instead of Neile. Winwood, whose attacks on the clergy two weeks earlier were believed to have angered Neile, also asked the House not to suspend business. Other members argued the merits of a protest directly to the King versus a protest to the Lords. After a lengthy debate, the House appointed a committee to seek proofs of their case against Neile and to recommend a course of action.

When the committee met the next day, it was able to

[9] *Commons jn.* i. 497.

determine what Neile had said in some detail, including the phrase *Noli me tangere* and the charge that the lower House was undutiful and seditious, even though there was no direct proof. The committee considered whether to ask the Lords about the truth of the report, to complain to the Lords and ask them for redress, or to ask the King for redress. Although there was little support for the first proposal among the committee members, they were badly divided between the last two. Finally they voted 21 to 18 in favour of seeking redress from the King. By a vote of 30 to 14 the committee recommended a 'forbearance' of all other business until they had an answer from the King.[10]

When the committee made this report to the House, most of the moderate opposition leaders opposed their recommendation. In a long speech Sir Edwin Sandys pointed out that the Commons would put the King in an embarrassing position. If he punished Neile himself, the Lords would be offended, but it would be undignified for him to have to beg the Lords to punish Neile. Sandys made a more telling point when he commented on the precedent which would be established. If the King could punish a member of the upper House on complaint of the Commons, he could also punish a member of the lower House on complaint of the Lords. Thus in the end the committee's proposal might be used to destroy the liberties of the lower House. Sandys gained the support of Digges, Sir Robert Phelips, Sir James Perrot, Sir Thomas Roe, and even Fuller and Hoskyns. At last Hakewill, who had made the report from the committee, was convinced of the danger. The principal supporter of an appeal to the King was Sir Roger Owen, but he was

[10] *Commons Debates 1621*, vii. 645-6; *H.M.C. Portland MSS*. ix. 133.

heckled so continually that he finally gave up. In the end the House resolved on a message to the Lords.

Phelips now proposed a forbearance of all other business. At this proposal the Speaker took the unusual step of speaking against the motion. He maintained that a 'forbearance' was really nothing less than a 'cessation' or adjournment, and the House of Commons could not adjourn while the Lords remained in session. But the House decided on their forbearance of all other business until the Lords had answered their message about Neile's speech.[11]

On Friday the 27th, Sir Roger Owen, a violent opponent of Neile, reported from the committee which had been appointed to draft a message to the Lords. After the message had been read, Sir George More, a strong supporter of the Crown, objected that the Commons had ordered a suspension of business until they received an answer from the Lords about Neile. But Owen's committee had decided that the suspension would last until the wrong was redressed. The House sent the message back for revision to the same committee, which was enlarged by the inclusion of several new members including Sir George More.

Meanwhile the House indulged in a bitter attack on Neile. Nicholas Fuller accused him of extorting money from the clergy of his diocese, of discriminating against ministers who preached twice in one day, and of suppressing Puritanical lectures on religion outside the regular church services. Neile was characterized as proud, contentious, and ungrateful to those who had helped him rise. He was even accused of sleeping through sermons. Finally the Speaker had to caution the House not to

[11] *Commons Debates 1621*, vii. 645-6; *H.M.C. Portland MSS.* ix. 133.

attack Neile without proof. The Commons then agreed on the message to be delivered to the Lords the next day, in which they declared that they would forbear all business until they had received an answer.[12]

The Speaker then read a letter from the King to the House. The King stated in his letter that he had heard of the Commons' cessation of business because they had received reports of Neile's speeches based only on rumour. The King reminded the House that little time remained for much important business. He also declared that he alone could summon and dissolve parliament, and asked the Commons to explain their cessation.

Sir George More seized the opportunity to propose that the House should continue with business of extraordinary importance, but his compromise fell flat. Various members of the opposition then attacked Winwood for misinforming the King about the intention of the Commons. Sir Samuel Sandys, who had been in parliament for thirty years, charged that sinister forces were at work to disrupt the session. Then he accused the Speaker of having shown the Commons' order book to the King. Speaker Crew was forced to admit that he had shown James a copy of the forbearance order. He explained that the King could see no difference between 'cessation' and 'forbearance' and declared that he desired to uphold the privileges of the House.[13]

The following day (Saturday, 28 May) the Commons drafted their answer to the King's letter. This reply was nothing more than a quibble of words. They declared that their suspension of business was not a cessation or recess, but only a forbearance, or the exercise of their

[12] *Commons Debates 1621*, vii. 646–7.
[13] Ibid.; *H.M.C. Portland MSS*. ix. 133–4.

right to prefer one matter of business to another. They failed to explain how they were exercising their preference when they brought all business to a halt. The Commons also declared that they would resume business just as soon as they were satisfied. The King replied to this message by summoning the Speaker and forty members of the Commons to an audience at Whitehall on Sunday afternoon. When the House appointed this committee, it took the extraordinary and significant step of excluding all the King's servants from it.

On Saturday also the Commons sent to the Lords their message containing a report of Neile's speeches, but refused to put it in writing. The Commons asked the Lords to join with them in some course that would yield satisfaction for the wrong done them and also stated that they would forbear from all other business until their message was answered. The Lords answered that they would make a definite reply as soon as possible. Meanwhile, despite pleas of individual members, the Commons remained firm in their resolution to suspend all business until they had received an answer from the Lords.[14]

Contemporary observers realized how serious the situation had become, and the events of the next few days did little to reassure them. But their worst fears were to be realized sooner, perhaps, than even they expected. When the Lords received the Commons' message about Neile on Saturday, 28 May, they began to consider their answer at once. The formerly solid block of privy councillors split over this issue. The Earl of Worcester, Lord Knollys, and Archbishop Abbot of Canterbury joined with Lord Rich and Viscount Lisle in demanding an explanation from Neile. But the Earls of Nottingham

[14] *H.M.C. Portland MSS.* ix. 134–5; *H.M.C. Hastings MSS.* iv. 267–8.

and Suffolk, and Lord Zouch objected to an oral accusation based only on rumour. Lord Chancellor Ellesmere, who had consulted the judges, held the same opinion. He declared that no peer would dare to speak freely in the upper House if he feared the Commons could call him to account for his words. Ellesmere also pointed out that only the members of the upper House could bear witness against Neile, but since they were his judges, they could not be his accusers also. At Ellesmere's suggestion the Lords decided to draft an answer on Monday saying that they could not proceed without more substantial proof of the charges against Neile.[15]

On Monday, 30 May, the Speaker reported to the House of Commons on his audience with the King at Whitehall the previous afternoon. The King was pleased that the lower House wanted to be cleared of charges of disloyalty, but he said that they were neglecting important business for a trivial matter. He warned them to be careful with precedents, for he might discover broad powers for the Crown by searching precedents. The King advised the Commons to continue with those matters for which he had summoned them, and he declared that he could not see the difference between a forbearance and a cessation. The Commons should not be so immature that they would refuse to do any business until they had gained one particular point, but they should take the opportunity to deal with matters of importance while there was still time. Instead of discussing an answer to the King's message, the Commons, urged on by John Glanville and Edward Alford, postponed it in accordance with their decision to abstain from all business except Neile's case.

[15] *H.M.C. Hastings MSS.* iv. 267–72.

The arrival of messengers from the upper House cut short the debate on this question. The messengers stated that the Lords would not take any action against Neile without proof of his words. Sir Edward Hoby, who had delivered the Commons' message to the Lords, stated that Bishop Neile had singled him out and had tearfully tried to excuse himself. Neile had declared that the words *Noli me tangere* applied only to himself, and had protested that he had never charged the Commons with seditious words or with striking at the root of the prerogative.

But the House was in no mood to accept Neile's penance. Sir William Cope, a strong Puritan, hinted that the Papists were trying to embroil parliament. He demanded that Neile should clear himself of the suspicion of Romanism. Although the more extreme members of the opposition like Sir Roger Owen and Sir Jerome Horsey wanted to continue the suspension of business, the saner counsels of Fuller, Alford, Sandys, and Sir Maurice Berkeley prevailed. The House appointed a committee to draft a new message to the Lords, and then returned to ordinary business.

On Tuesday the last day of May this committee drafted a new message to the Lords while the House of Commons proceeded with routine matters. Sir Roger Owen reported to the House from this committee. Owen declared that even though the first message had accomplished nothing, a second message might have better results. Because the committee believed that they could not offer better proof to the Lords, the second message was the same as the first, with the addition that the Lords knew what had been said in their own House. The message also stated that if the Lords refused to punish Neile, they should inform the Commons that the charge against him was false. The Commons appointed Sir Roger Owen, one of their most hot-headed members, to deliver the message, and then proceeded with routine business.[16]

When the Lords received this message, they answered that they would reply the same day if possible. By this time almost all of the lords had deserted Neile. Even the Earl of Nottingham joined with Archbishop Abbot, Lord Spencer, and Lord Saye in asking him for an explanation. Only the Earl of Suffolk and Bishop Bilson of Winchester attempted to protect Neile. Finally, after the Earl of Southampton had affirmed the unanimity of the House, Neile rose to make his defence. With a great show of emotion and even tears he tried to excuse himself. He paraded his humble origin and personal poverty, but made no real defence. In substance he said that he had not intended to offend the Lords or to displease the Commons. Without attempting any detailed explanation of his words, he stated that he was willing to give satisfaction to either House.

Lord Knollys, a privy councillor, now spoke in Neile's defence. He declared that the Lords were not obliged to render an account to the Commons of what took place in the upper House, and expressed the hope that the Lords would accept Neile's explanation and submission. The Earl of Suffolk, another councillor, condemned the Commons for attacking Neile's character. He also declared that he would have accused the Commons of attacking the prerogative if they had questioned impositions. But other peers, including Lord Chandos and the Earl of Southampton, felt that Neile should admit that he had

[16] *H.M.C. Portland MSS.* ix. 135; *Commons Debates 1621*, vii. 647–9.

spoken the offending words. At last Neile denied that he had spoken them, but he declared that he would make any submission ordered by the Lords.

In their reply to the Commons, the Lords stated that Neile had declared with tears in his eyes that he had spoken nothing of evil intent against the lower House. He protested that he had been misinterpreted, and that his words had been strained far beyond what he had intended. The Lords declared that they had accepted Neile's explanation and that they would have punished him if they thought that he had cast any aspersions on the lower House. The Lords concluded their message with the statement that they had satisfied the Commons on this occasion in order to expedite the King's business, but in the future they would not allow a member of their House to be accused by rumour alone.[17]

Here the whole matter might well have ended, but by this time the temper of the Commons had reached a fever pitch. Rumours were rife that some cunning hand was working behind the scenes to disrupt the parliament. With good reason Chamberlain became progressively gloomier about the results of the session. The atmosphere of the lower House was so tense and so charged with suspicion that the best of friends were affected. On Tuesday, 31 May, Sir Edwin Sandys and Sir Dudley Digges, two pillars of the opposition who had 'hitherto agreed like sworn brethren', quarrelled so violently that Digges complained to the House.[18] Although this breach was soon healed, it was indicative of the atmosphere in the Commons. The accusations against Neile had gone to such extremes that even obscure members, who revelled

[17] *H.M.C. Hastings MSS.* iv. 273–7.
[18] *Letters of Chamberlain*, i. 535–7.

in such excitement, had begun to find them distasteful. The Commons were becoming so ungovernable that even their chosen leaders were losing the power to guide them on any sensible course.

Chapter X

The Earl of Northampton as it were in Triumph

THE reply of the Lords explaining away Bishop Neile's speeches served only to arouse the Commons still more and hasten what was by this time wellnigh inevitable—an angry and bitter dissolution. Although the Commons received this message on Tuesday, 31 May, the hour was so late that a general debate was postponed until Wednesday.

On Wednesday Sir Roger Owen opened the debate with another bitter attack on Neile. He was unmoved by the bishop's tears, and declared that the Commons should be given the opportunity to judge of Neile's words for themselves since the Lords did not deny that he had said them. He also criticized the upper House for suggesting how the Commons should proceed, and favoured a new committee to consider the next move against Neile. Although Sir Walter Chute, the King's carver, hinted at the danger of a dissolution, other members joined in the attack on Neile and suggested a message to the King. Sir Thomas Roe, who had previously exerted a moderating influence, was especially bitter. He proposed that the Commons should enter an order to disable Neile 'ether to be aboute the kinge or to be a bushop or to be amongest reasonable men, but to runne awaye and bewayle his estate in the woodes amongest wilde beastes'.[1]

The House then got on the trail of a recusant, one

[1] *Commons Debates 1621*, vii. 649–50.

Francis Lovett, to whom Neile was said to have given a certificate of conformity in return for a bribe, even though Lovett had not received Communion or taken the oaths of supremacy and allegiance. As Lovett was believed to be in London, a warrant was issued to three members of the House to apprehend him, but they returned empty-handed the same afternoon. They reported that although they had missed Lovett at the Swann Inn in the Strand, where he had spent the night, they were told he was dining with John Thornborough, the Bishop of Bristol. They then proceeded to the bishop's residence. When his servants refused to tell them who was dining with their master, two of them, Duncombe and Watson, went boldly up to Thornborough's dining room and demanded Lovett.

. . . the bushop was much discontented and angrye, whereuppon Watson tolde him he was a Justice of peace, and might searche of his owne authoritie, the bushop answered fiddle faddle, if I were not a bushop, I tell you to your teeth. . . .[2]

Balked in their attempt to seize Lovett, they did return with a man who knew him. Their witness deposed that Lovett had paid Neile a pound for his certificate of conformity, but had not taken the two oaths. The witness also stated that Lovett, who had been imprisoned in Warwickshire as a recusant, had subsequently moved into Buckinghamshire to be in the diocese of Lincoln, where Neile was the bishop. Sir Thomas Lake now reported that the King had sent for Neile because he was so concerned about Lovett. Lake added that the King had ordered an examination of the book which was signed

[2] Ibid. 650–1.

by those taking the oath of allegiance, and that Lovett's signature appeared.

The next time that the Commons met (Friday, 3 June)[3] a message from Lovett was read in the House. While Lovett admitted that he had not received Communion, he declared that he had taken the oaths. This message appears to have mollified the House. After Lovett had repeated his statement at the bar of the House the same day, his case was dropped because a more important matter had come before the Commons.[4]

This new development was a message from the King which struck the lower House like a bombshell. First, he told them to prepare a bill for the continuance of statutes and also such other bills as they thought advisable. Then he informed the Commons that unless they granted him supply quickly and effectually, parliament would be dissolved on Thursday, 9 June, less than a week away.

This message affected the members of the House in different ways. Some, seeing their reign nearing its end,

[3] The Commons had voted on Wednesday by 248 to 141 not to meet on Thursday, 1 June, because it was Ascension Day. This vote is an interesting commentary on Puritanism in the House of Commons in 1614. Certainly a staunchly Puritan House would have decided to meet on Ascension Day. The very size of the margin in a large House indicates that its Puritanism has been over-emphasized. No doubt many members of the House wanted to reform ecclesiastical abuses, and almost all of them were haunted by fears of Popery. But the majority would have been satisfied with reforms which would not have changed the Establishment drastically. The House of Lords agreed not to meet on Ascension Day without debate or division. Holles in *H.M.C. Portland MSS.* ix. 135-6 gave the division as 248 to 191, but such a full House seems unlikely. In the only other two divisions recorded, 305 and 334 (or 354) voted against 439 on this issue according to Holles's figures and 389 according to the *Commons jn.* out of about 472 members. It is also significant that while only 305 members were present on 31 May, when nothing of great importance was debated, attendance jumped to at least 389 on 1 June when the Lords' answer about Neile was taken up.

[4] *Commons Debates 1621*, vii. 649-51; *H.M.C. Portland MSS.* ix. 135.

moderated their conduct. But the majority, far from being cowed, became more violent than ever. For the few remaining days of the session the Commons was completely beyond the control of anyone.[5]

When the King's message was received, the supporters of the Crown made one more attempt to salvage the session. Sir George More maintained that a dissolution would harm both the King and his subjects because they were all members of the same commonwealth. Sir Julius Caesar proposed a committee on supply, and defended the legality of the King's stand on impositions. Sir Thomas Lake also warned the House that parliament would be dissolved unless supply was voted at once.

A number of other members supported the officials. Francis Ashley urged the Commons to relieve the King's wants. He also suggested that they should determine how impositions could be tested again before the courts of law. Sir James Perrot suggested a committee to consider supply and impositions together. Even Sir Thomas Roe and Thomas Wentworth, the Oxford Puritan, joined in the proposal for an immediate grant of supply.

But other members stood firm in the face of the King's message. Christopher Neville, a younger son of Lord Bergavenny and no relation to Sir Henry Neville, delivered a curious speech drafted for some other occasion. Neville, who was a young man straight from school, strung together all the appropriate Latin quotations that he could find, repeating, 'O tempora! O mores!' over and over again like a parrot. He also attacked the courtiers, criticized impositions, and made disparaging remarks about the bills of grace. Although this speech

[5] *Commons Debates 1621*, vii. 651; *H.M.C. Portland MSS.* ix. 136; *Letters of Chamberlain*, i. 537–9.

merely amused his audience, it had dire consequences for the orator.

John Hoskyns made the most threatening speech of all. He declared, in an obvious reference to Somerset and the swarm of Scots around the King, that a wise prince would send the strangers home as Canute had done with his Danish followers when he became King of England. Hoskyns then made an ominous and threatening allusion to the Sicilian Vespers. Sir William Strode urged the House to petition the King on impositions. Nicholas Fuller and John Whitson supported him and attacked the Papists. Nicholas Hyde protested that impositions were illegal and also condemned the King's extravagance. The House finally decided to meet in the afternoon as a committee of the whole to consider how they might pacify the King, but refused to be stampeded into voting supply.[6]

The officials tried blunt tactics again in the afternoon at the committee which was drafting a reply to the King. Winwood and Lake declared that the King did not want an answer to his message. They stated that there were only two choices before the Commons. If they did not grant supply, the King would dissolve parliament. But despite this warning, the committee proceeded with its deliberations, and appointed a sub-committee to draft a reply by the following morning.

But on Saturday morning (4 June) the Speaker sent word that he was in bed with the mumps. Perhaps he feigned illness and absented himself in the expectation that the Commons would not meet. The government may

[6] *H.M.C. Portland MSS.* ix. 136, 138; Smith, *Life and Letters of Wotton,* ii. 36–39; *Letters of Chamberlain,* i. 537–9; P.R.O. S.P. Venice 99/16, ff. 104–5.

have believed that the lower House would come round to their point of view after a breathing-space of two days.

In any case the Commons did assemble on Saturday without the Speaker, and discussed their message to the King. In this message they acknowledged with all humility that the King possessed the exclusive right to summon and dissolve parliament, and they stated that they would be content with his decision, whatever it might be. But they protested that they could not satisfy him as they had intended when they were so pressed for time unless they received satisfaction in regard to impositions. They stated that there were far more impositions now than in earlier times, and that the King had declared in parliament on two occasions his inherited right to levy them. They feared that they would confirm the right to impose forever and would wrong the country if they granted supply to the King while the question remained unsettled. The Commons concluded by offering a grant to the King if he would cancel impositions. The House then chose forty members to deliver this message to the King on Monday.[7]

James was badly frightened by the wild and irresponsible speeches delivered on Friday. Hoskyns's speech in particular aroused a neurotic fear that his enemies were plotting to assassinate his Scottish favourites and perhaps even himself. At this juncture the King took the extraordinary step of turning to Sarmiento, the Spanish ambassador, for advice. Sir John Digby, who had been the English ambassador in Spain, had already assured James that the King of Spain would be his firm and true friend in this crisis. Sarmiento confirmed all that Digby had told James so amply that the King was encouraged to reject

[7] *Commons Debates 1621*, vii. 651–2; *H.M.C. Portland MSS*. ix. 136.

contrary advice from other quarters and dissolve parliament.[8]

The King also sought elsewhere for encouragement. The day after Hoskyns's speech he consulted the aged Earl of Northampton, who, it must be remembered, was the leader of the Spanish faction on the council and an opponent of parliament from the beginning. Northampton had an excellent reason for advising James to dissolve parliament: indirectly he had incited Hoskyns to deliver his attack on the Scots, anticipating that the speech would panic the King and precipitate the dissolution. Hoskyns himself seems to have been simply the tool of the pro-Spanish interests. He was not well versed in history and did not realise the implications of his reference to the Sicilian Vespers. This part of his speech, in fact, was suggested to him by one Dr. Lionel Sharpe and Sir Charles Cornwallis, both of whom were Northampton's tools. They promised Hoskyns the protection of Northampton and perhaps of the Earl of Somerset as well in case he was questioned about the speech, and they probably gave him the additional inducement of £20 cash.[9]

Under the influence of Sarmiento and Northampton James took courage and determined to dissolve parliament. Although the commission was dated Monday, 7 June, it is reported to have been signed on Sunday. However, the decision was certainly made on Saturday, for

[8] F. Francisco de Jesus, *Narrative of the Spanish Marriage Treaty*, pp. 286-7.

[9] *Court and Times of James I*, i. 323-4; *Letters of Chamberlain*, i. 540-3; Smith, *Life and Letters of Wotton*, ii. 38-39; Osborn, *Life, Letters, and Writings of John Hoskyns*, p. 75; P.R.O. Spanish transcripts 12/35 (Sarmiento to Philip III, 20/30 June 1614); P.R.O. 99/16, ff. 104-5 (Venice correspondence); P.R.O. S.P. Dom. 14/77:42.

messengers were sent to the lodgings of peers in London and Westminster that evening asking them to be in the parliament house in their robes at eight o'clock on Monday morning for the dissolution.[10]

As soon as the news was out, Winwood and Lord Chancellor Ellesmere tried desperately to save the situation. But all that they could obtain was a letter from the King postponing the dissolution for a single day. They were so late in gaining even this slight respite that the King signed the letter in bed on Monday morning.

When the Commons met the same day, they knew that the commission to dissolve parliament had been signed. In fact the Lords sent word to them that they were sitting in their robes waiting for instructions to execute the commission. The Speaker also read a letter from the King to the House. Although the King did not demand a vote of supply, he reminded the Commons that they had been in session for two months, the usual period for parliaments in the past. He also stated that supply should come at this time because its proper place was at the end of a session. Although he had previously decided to dissolve parliament on the following Thursday, he had now changed his mind. But he would suspend until Tuesday his commission for dissolving parliament immediately.

The supporters of the Crown now made an attempt to save the session from utter failure. They proposed a message to the King which would acknowledge his grace and would ask him to continue the session if they promised a liberal grant of supply. Various officials then tried to persuade the House to adopt their plan. The king's serjeant, Sir Henry Montague, reported that the

[10] H.M.C. Portland MSS. ix. 136; H.M.C. Hastings MSS. iv. 280; Commons Debates 1621, vii. 653.

King and his learned counsel agreed that impositions could be levied only on imports and exports, not on internal trade. Winwood now made a last attempt to save the situation. He declared that only an immediate grant of supply would persuade the King to prorogue parliament instead of dissolving it. He also pointed out that foreign affairs were critical, and that England's trade would suffer unless the King had money for negotiations with Russia. The treasurer of the navy, Sir Robert Mansell, supported Winwood's arguments.

Sir Edwin Sandys replied to the officials in a long and doleful speech. He declared that the King's claim to levy impositions threatened the security of property and the liberties of parliament, and a grant of supply at this time would imply an acknowledgement of the King's power to impose. Sandys suggested that they should ask the King to continue the session and allow parliament, the ancient judge of the liberties of the kingdom, to decide the impositions question. Then, on their part, the Commons would make an immediate grant of supply.

The House held a long debate on these proposals. The knowledge of the impending dissolution caused much confusion, and the Commons had never been more disorderly, with many members acting like roaring boys instead of wise councillors. In the end the House appointed a committee to redraft Sandys's proposals in a milder and more palatable form.

A rumour had already reached the House that some of its members would be charged with seditious speeches after the dissolution. When Sir Henry Wotton demanded an explanation of Hoskyns's reference to the Sicilian Vespers, Hoskyns managed to convince the House that he had intended no sedition. But Hoskyns was soon to learn that a vote of the Commons was too frail a protection against the King.[11]

At the same time the House of Lords was debating the question of executing the commission to dissolve parliament. When they met on Monday morning, everything was prepared for the dissolution. The peers were robed, and the commission lay on the table, with the benches for the commissioners already in place.

After a long silence the lord chancellor spoke. He announced that the King had issued a commission to dissolve parliament on this day. But if the Lords expected a message from the lower House and wanted to postpone the execution of the commission until the next day, he would agree, provided the other commissioners gave their consent. Although the Earl of Suffolk believed that they could not delay the execution of the commission, the Earl of Southampton declared that the question concerned only the commissioners. At his suggestion the commissioners retired to the lord chancellor's chamber, where they conferred for half an hour. When they returned, the lord chancellor announced that the commissioners were willing to delay the execution of their commission until the next day.

The Lords then sent a message to the Commons that they would not act on the dissolution until Tuesday in the hope that the lower House would take some step to grant supply. The Commons replied that they had received a letter from the King postponing the dissolution until Tuesday. After the Lords had waited for several hours without receiving any further message from the Commons, they informed the latter that they would

[11] *H.M.C. Portland MSS.* ix. 137; *Commons Debates 1621*, vii. 652–4; *Letters of Chamberlain*, i. 537–9.

adjourn until two o'clock on Tuesday (the next day), and that they would expect an answer from the Commons at that time.[12]

The House of Commons met as usual on Tuesday, 7 June. The draft of their latest message to the King varied only slightly from Sandys's proposals. But the House demanded security for the hearing on impositions, and they stated in strong terms that this question was outside the jurisdiction of the judges.

A final attempt at a compromise was now made. Sir Maurice Berkeley asked the House to grant supply in gratitude for the King's graces. John Hoskyns suggested a grant of subsidies on condition that the money should be returned if impositions were not cancelled by October. Sir Herbert Croft suggested an immediate grant accompanied by a declaration of the security of property.

But other members opposed any compromise despite the imminence of the dissolution. Francis Ashley suggested a committee for supply on a definite date, so that grievances could be presented to the King in the meantime. He still maintained that the subsidies granted should be in proportion to the grievances redressed. Sir William Walter flatly opposed any grant made for fear of a dissolution. The question was hotly debated until three o'clock, with the majority in favour of a committee on supply in the traditional manner.[13]

In the meantime the Lords had assembled, and the commissioners' bench had been set in place. After some time had elapsed and the Commons did not appear, the Lords sent a message to summon them for the dissolution. When it became clear to Winwood and his colleagues

[12] *H.M.C. Hastings MSS.* iv. 280–2; *Commons Debates 1621,* vii. 654.
[13] *Commons Debates 1621,* vii. 654–6; *H.M.C. Portland MSS.* ix. 137.

in the Commons that no subsidies would be voted without a delay, they asked the Lords whether the commissioners were obliged to dissolve parliament or also had the authority to continue it. When the three privy councillors returned to the lower House without an answer, the Speaker tried to put the subsidy to a vote, but the Commons flatly refused to act.

By this time the lord chancellor had realized that the dissolution could not be avoided. As soon as the Lords had donned their robes, the Commons were summoned. The commissioners sat on a long bench, with the Archbishop of Canterbury in the centre and the lord chancellor on his right. After the clerk had read the commission in Latin, the lord chancellor declared that according to its terms this assembly was to be no parliament, but it was dissolved and annihilated as though no such thing had ever been. Thus, on Tuesday, 7 June 1614, at about three o'clock in the afternoon the second parliament of King James came to its end after existing for almost exactly two months. The day after the dissolution the Earl of Northampton, who had lain ill in Greenwich, paraded through London gallantly attended by forty followers on horseback 'as yt were in triumphe with only Sir Charles Cornwallis [who had suborned Hoskyns] beside him in his coach'. Northampton did not long outlive his triumph, dying a week later from a tumour in the thigh.[14]

This parliament was dissolved in this particular manner so that certain statutes should remain in force which would otherwise have lapsed if it had been a lawful parliament. Because the Palatine bill had passed through both Houses and had been confirmed by the King, there was

[14] *H.M.C. Hastings MSS.* iv. 282–3; *H.M.C. Portland MSS.* iv. 137–8; *Letters of Chamberlain*, i. 540–3.

some question whether or not the meeting had actually been a session of parliament, but in the end the form of the dissolution was not challenged. The nickname 'addled' for this parliament must have been in common use shortly after the dissolution, for Lorkin used it (in the form 'addle') on 18 June and again on 11 September. The name obviously referred to the fact that no legislation had resulted from the session.[15]

The Crown was prepared for quick action after the dissolution. On Wednesday, the day after parliament was dissolved, the King returned from Greenwich by water and summoned a meeting of his council. Warrants had already been dispatched for the arrest of various members of the lower House, who were called before the council at this time. When they appeared at the council-table, the King watched the proceedings secretly through an aperture in the hangings. Those who had been assigned parts in the conference on impositions had to produce all their notes and papers, which were burned. A day or so later the King expressed his indignation at parliament by tearing up all its bills and papers publicly in the banqueting chamber at Whitehall.

But the King's actions were not confined to such innocuous measures. Four members of the lower House, Hoskyns, Chute, Christopher Neville, and Thomas Wentworth of Oxford, were summoned before the council, charged with seditious speeches, and sent to the Tower. Sir Charles Cornwallis and Dr. Lionel Sharpe were imprisoned the following Monday on the charge that they had incited Hoskyns. Sir John Savile, Sir Roger Owen, Sir Edward Giles, Sir James Perrot, and Sir Edwin Sandys were ordered to remain in London, but by

[15] *H.M.C. Portland MSS.* ix. 138; *Court and Times of James I,* i. 323, 346.

10 July they had all been discharged. Owen, Nicholas Hyde, and others were struck off the rolls of justices of the peace.[16]

As to the other six, the most serious offenders were Hoskyns, Cornwallis, and Sharpe. Christopher Neville was imprisoned for his schoolboyish attack on the Court. But on making his submission, he found some favour and was removed from the Tower to the Fleet before the end of June. Neville secured his release on 10 July. Wentworth was charged with quoting the book of Daniel against impositions and with citing the assassination of Henry IV of France as a case of Divine judgement, but he was regarded as foolish instead of dangerous. Wentworth, who was imprisoned mainly to satisfy the French ambassador, secured his release on 29 June, once the ambassador had declared himself satisfied. Sir Walter Chute suffered because he attacked impositions even though he was carver to the King. Also the King may have felt that he had acted as a tale-bearer for the opposition, and perhaps a letter which he wrote to the King justifying his conduct exasperated James still further. Chute, who was not released until 2 October, also lost his place and was confined to the vicinity of his father's house.[17]

The King dealt severely with Hoskyns, Sharpe, and Cornwallis for their part in disrupting parliament. All three remained in prison until June 1615, when they were all released after signing submissions. But the King's resentment pursued Hoskyns even farther. When he was elected mayor of Hereford, his old constituency, in the

---

[16] *H.M.C. Portland MSS.* ix. 138–9; *Liber famelicus of Sir James Whitelocke*, pp. 41–43; *Letters of Chamberlain*, i. 540–3; P.R.O. Spanish transcripts 12/35 (Sarmiento to Philip III, 20/30 June 1614).

[17] *H.M.C. Portland MSS.* ix. 138; P.R.O. Paris transcripts 3/48 (Puysieux to Buisseaux 30 June/10 July and 18/28 June 1614).

summer of 1616, the King refused to allow him to serve and forced the corporation to make a new choice. But in good time even Hoskyns was restored to favour. He became a serjeant in 1623 and ultimately a member of the Council of the Marches.[18]

Sir Edward Phelips, the master of the rolls, also felt the King's wrath. Not only was his son Sir Robert a leading figure in the opposition, but also Hoskyns was his close friend. In spite of his position the King suspected that Sir Edward was involved with Hoskyns because he was jealous of Winwood. Some observers felt that the chief cause of Phelips's death in September 1614 was grief over his disgrace.[19]

On the other hand, some supporters of the Crown received prompt rewards. Despite the dismal failure of the parliament, no blame fell on the Speaker. In fact the King was so pleased with his services that before the end of June he was knighted and created a serjeant. Several other members of the lower House also became serjeants about the same time, including the Queen's attorney-general, Sir Robert Hitcham, Leonard Bawtrey, Henry Finch, Francis Moore, and William Towse.[20]

Royal favour was extended even farther for the King's supporters. Robert Wolverston, who sat for Cardigan borough in 1614, took no recorded part in the session. Yet he so impressed the King with the value of his services in the Commons that in August and October 1614 James intervened for him in a case before Chancery. At least two royal letters to Lord Chancellor Ellesmere instructed him to show Wolverston all possible considera-

[18] B.M. Add. MSS. 11053, f. 77.
[19] *Liber famelicus of Sir James Whitelocke*, p. 43; *Court and Times of James I*, i. 325–9.
[20] *Court and Times of James I*, i. 325–9.

tion. Clearly service to the Crown in parliament had material rewards. But whatever rewards were given to the King's supporters and whatever punishment was meted out to his opponents, the failure of the parliament left him facing serious problems aggravated by the events of the session.[21]

[21] Collier (ed.), *Egerton Papers*, pp. 463–5.

Chapter XI

The Addled Parliament and Royal Policy

THE dissolution of the Addled Parliament left the financial crisis farther from a solution than ever. Early in 1614 the council had reluctantly concluded that the Crown could avoid bankruptcy only through a parliamentary grant, and now that hope was dashed. Also the treasury had been thrown into confusion by the death of the Earl of Northampton, the chief commissioner of the treasury, and the King was urged to appoint a treasurer as the first step. Meanwhile the chief problem was to meet daily expenses, for the royal coffers were almost bare of hard cash.

The first ray of hope in this desperate situation came from the bishops. Perhaps sensible of Neile's responsibility for the dissolution, or grateful to the King for his steadfast support of episcopacy, they decided to offer the Crown a free gift in the form of the best piece of plate possessed by each bishop. While some presented the plate itself, others redeemed their gifts with sums of money. Their example was followed by many nobles, the privy councillors, many officials, and some of the judges. Most of these presents were in cash. Among others, Suffolk, Somerset, Salisbury, Hertford, and Winwood made contributions. Although Coke made a handsome present of some £200, his colleagues were niggardly. One judge offered as little as £20, which was refused. Some at Court hoped that the total would be large, but others were pessimistic of the sum that would be contributed.

This spontaneous contribution by Court circles suggested to the government the idea of a nation-wide benevolence on similar terms. Meanwhile Winwood approached the London merchants in the King's name. Anticipating his move, they offered a voluntary contribution of 5,000 marks, which was refused. On 26 June 1614 Winwood asked them to lend the Crown £100,000. They now raised their offer of a free gift to £10,000, and in the end escaped the loan by this means.

Meanwhile the Crown, realizing the ill feeling which the dissolution had engendered, decided to grant by proclamation many of the graces offered to parliament. It was hoped that this move would stimulate the collection of the benevolence. Among other graces the King granted partial exemption from the Council of Wales to the border counties, and prohibited secret inquiries to determine the Crown's claim to land. Some steps were also taken to codify the law.

By early July the council had sent letters to the sheriff and justices of the peace of every shire requesting a benevolence. These letters, which included a list of the contributors at Court, instructed the sheriffs and justices to publish the information. A list of the contributors in every shire was to be sent to the King, and the success of the proposal in each county was declared to be an indication of the zeal and loyalty of the sheriff and justices. Finally, the letter stated that the money would be used solely to pay the Crown's debts.

Although the government had hoped that the contributions would at least equal two subsidies, the benevolence was no great success, and the amount collected fell far short of the goal. While a single subsidy of the laity was £68,000, both clergy and laity contributed only

£66,100 to the benevolence. Of this sum £23,500 came from the City of London, the bishops, and the courtiers. The remainder of the country contributed only £42,600 altogether.

On 10 July 1614 Northampton's nephew, the Earl of Suffolk, became lord treasurer, but the substitution of one Howard for another did little to improve matters. Indeed in 1618 Suffolk was finally removed from office for gross irregularities in his conduct of treasury business. Once it became obvious that the benevolence would not come up to expectations, Suffolk's solution for the financial problem was to multiply the money-raising projects resorted to between 1610 and 1614.

Among other schemes a commission was set up to survey all buildings erected within seven miles of London since 1603 contrary to various proclamations. The government anticipated that the owners would pay fines rather than remove the buildings, but the Crown realized little profit because many of the owners were too poor to pay. On the other hand, the project aroused much resentment because the commission proceeded as severely against houses surrounded by ample acreage as against those crowded together. A second scheme was a levy of 2d. per barrel on beer in lieu of its seizure to supply the royal household. This levy was bitterly resented, for men realized clearly that the two pence could become two shillings, and that such exactions had no limit.

Although similar projects abounded, they produced little cash. Late in 1614 affairs reached such a state that almost no royal officials, not even the humblest, were paid, and there was talk of cancelling all pensions. But gradually Sir Lionel Cranfield, who had become surveyor-general of the customs in 1613, extended his influence over government finances. After Suffolk's fall in 1618 Cranfield became the dominant figure in financial administration and by careful management slowly improved the Crown's position. The overall deficit, which stood at £150,000 in 1617, was reduced to £100,000 in 1618. With the increase in customs revenue which came from growing commercial prosperity, Cranfield balanced the ordinary budget in 1618, and for 1619 looked forward to a surplus of £45,000 in the ordinary accounts. At this time the Crown's debts amounted to £726,000. Barring a crisis calling for a vast increase in expenditures, after 1618 the King could anticipate a better financial position than he had enjoyed for almost a decade.

Despite the dismal failure of the Addled Parliament, rumours of a new session were rife almost before its members had left Westminster. On 2 July 1614 Lorkin reported this news to a friend. Although he was sceptical of any result, he had gone so far as to talk to various persons about a seat for his correspondent in the new House of Commons. A few days later Chamberlain also mentioned rumours of a session during the next winter.

But little more was heard of a new parliament until the following summer. By June 1615 the King was in more desperate straits than ever, but the old factions in the council hampered any decision. Although a parliament seemed to be the only solution to the problem, the Spanish faction opposed it, fearing that the Commons would demand war with Spain as the price of financial support. The two strongest opponents of a parliament were Suffolk and Somerset, who feared that their plundering of the public treasury would be revealed.

By early September the rumour was abroad again, this time with some basis in fact. Late in that month the council spent several days considering the whole question of finance. One by one the councillors expressed their views. Lake, Caesar, Parry, Coke, Winwood, Lord Wotton, Lord Knollys, Lord Zouch, Bishop Andrewes of Ely, Fenton, Exeter, Pembroke, Lennox, and Archbishop Abbot of Canterbury were all heartily in favour of a parliament. But Nottingham, Suffolk, and Lord Chancellor Ellesmere gave only grudging approval, and spoke of the difficulty of settling the old question of impositions.

Apparently the Spanish faction continued to work on the King behind the scenes. In spite of the apparent unanimity in the council, both Sarmiento and the Venetian ambassador were convinced of the Spanish ascendancy at Court. About the same time Bacon advised the King to summon parliament, as he had done in 1613. In general his advice followed his earlier memorandum, but it included a severe condemnation of undertaking as well. No parliament was summoned as a result of all this activity. Whatever chance there may have been for a session at this time disappeared when in October of 1615 the King's attention was diverted to the Overbury case, which kept the Court in a turmoil until the following spring. Even when the hue and cry after Somerset had died down, popular feeling was so aroused against the Court that the time was inopportune for a parliament.

Somehow or other the royal treasury dragged on through 1616 and 1617 without actually becoming bankrupt. Although contemporaries could see little hope of solvency unless parliament was summoned, the government did nothing. The Spanish faction, still fearful of the strength of public opinion, was able to resist all demands for a session of parliament. When Lake was appointed joint secretary early in 1616, the Spanish faction became more influential than ever, but opposition to a parliament came partly from the King himself. Nevertheless, in early 1617 it was rumoured that the Spanish marriage negotiation was simply a lever to force parliament to grant supply. The whole report of an impending session, however, dissolved by the autumn of 1617.[1]

Before another year was out, however, a crisis which in the end would force the King into action was developing on the Continent. When James's son-in-law Frederick accepted the crown of Bohemia and thereby precipitated a general European war, a session of the English parliament became almost inevitable. James was assured of the support of the Commons for the defence of Protestantism and for the protection of the heritage of his daughter's husband.

But still the King hesitated, postponing parliament until November 1620. His reluctance arose partly from memories of 1610 and 1614, and partly from the fear that once parliament met, his favourite scheme of a Spanish marriage would be ruined. Finally with the greatest reluctance, when he realized the threat to the Palatinate itself, the King summoned parliament on 6 November 1620.

Throughout the period from June of 1614 to November of 1620, several interrelated factors had combined to postpone a parliament. One of these factors was a

---

[1] *Cal. S.P. Venice 1613–15*, pp. 512–13; *Cal. S.P. Venice 1615–17*, pp. 12–13, 33–34, 37–38, 43–45, 88–89, 116–17, 165, 570–2, 585–7; P.R.O. S.P. Dom. 14/81:115; 14/83:68; 14/93:134; P.R.O. Spanish transcripts 12/36 (Sarmiento to Lerma 21 June/1 July, 18/28 July, and 29 Sept./8 Oct. 1615); 12/37 (Sarmiento to Philip III, 20/30 Jan. 1616); 12/38 ('Memorandum of the feigned names which are used in England'); Spedding, *Letters and Life of Bacon*, v. 176–91.

succession of events which would have interfered with a session. Early in 1615 the Irish parliament met, and from the end of that year well into 1616 the Overbury case kept the Court in a turmoil. The King's visit to Scotland in 1617 and the uproar over Raleigh's execution in 1618 disrupted the normal course of events and made a concurrent session of the English parliament difficult if not entirely impossible.

When 1618 was reached, a second factor, Spanish influence at Court, became closely involved with the first. One reason for its success was purely personal. Count Gondomar (still Sarmiento in 1614), the Spanish ambassador, acquired a remarkable ascendancy over the King, and his influence was strengthened by the consistently pro-Spanish attitude of the powerful Howard family. Also, the King had in his mind the scheme for a general pacification of Europe by a great Anglo-Spanish agreement based on a royal marriage alliance. This revolution in international politics would reconcile Protestant and Catholic, and would elevate James to the position of the peacemaker and arbiter of Europe.

The great flaw in this scheme was that everyone except the King realized that he was a pawn in the hands of Spain. The Spanish government was quite willing to go along with James as long as his policy served their ends. But they did not for one instant consider making any major concessions to the English. The aim of Spanish policy in England was to secure English neutrality while Spain gained its ends by force or intrigue. The point which some contemporaries misunderstood was the King's sincerity in the Spanish marriage negotiations. Although an ample dowry might have freed him from dependence on parliament for a time, he had no intention of using the Spanish marriage as a threat to force parliament to grant supply.

Whether or not the full significance of Spanish diplomacy was clearly realized in England, after 1614 public opinion was bitterly and increasingly hostile to Spain. While the Spanish threat to Protestantism may have been exaggerated, the popular detestation of Spain served the same ends, whatever its cause. It was clear throughout this period that if parliament met, it would be so violently anti-Spanish that it might force the King into war against Spain.

This situation compelled Gondomar to forestall a session of parliament in his master's interest. The Howards and their allies had the same end in view. While the King had no reason to promote Spanish policy as such, his great international scheme would have been ruined by a breach with Spain. So Gondomar worked on the King and through the Howards to prevent parliament from meeting. After Raleigh's execution no specific internal problem lay in the path of a parliament. But events in Germany beginning in 1618 inflamed public opinion against Spain more strongly than ever. The King was torn between his duty toward his relatives and his faith in his great experiment in 'kingcraft' on an international scale.

A third factor working against parliament was more subtle. With the utter failure of the Addled Parliament James's faith in parliamentary institutions was badly shaken. He now felt that the Commons were too unruly, factious, and headstrong to recognize the reasonableness and wisdom of his leadership. With co-operation impossible because of the wilfulness of his opponents, he would do well to dispense with parliament entirely.

But the events of early 1620 shook the King's resolution, even though he still tried all possible expedients before he came to a decision. Finally, when no other means of raising money remained, and it was clear that Frederick was faced with the loss of the Palatinate as well as Bohemia, James reluctantly summoned a parliament.

The events of 1614 were still so clear in the King's mind that only this threat to the position of his daughter could drive him to take a step which threatened all his grandiose plans. While the rush of events and the Spanish influence might have prevented him from summoning parliament earlier, the strife and bitterness of the Addled Parliament were powerful arguments in favour of his policy of personal rule after 1614.

Chapter XII

The Addled Parliament and the Opposition

THE Addled Parliament was not the isolated event that the chronology of the early Stuart period might indicate. Although it lasted only two months and the next parliament was not summoned for almost seven years, the continuity of development was unbroken. The proportion of new members in the Addled Parliament was not extraordinary if the ten-year lapse since the elections of 1604 is considered. Likewise, the number of members who served in later parliaments compares favourably with the figures for Elizabethan parliaments. Also, the Addled Parliament showed no important variation from Elizabethan parliaments in the occupations, station, and background of the members. The majority were gentry, with lawyers, merchants, and officials forming smaller groups. A somewhat higher proportion, but not significantly so, had been educated at one of the universities or at the inns of court. In its composition the Addled Parliament showed no contrast to earlier or later parliaments.

This continuity is demonstrated not only by statistics, but also by a continuity of leadership in the opposition. Sir Edwin Sandys, Nicholas Fuller, Sir Roger Owen, and others took a leading part in the parliament of 1604. The influence of members of the Addled Parliament was even more pronounced in the stormy parliaments of the 1620's. Sandys, Sir Dudley Digges, William Hakewill, and Edward Alford all sat in 1621, and at least one of this group sat in every parliament of that decade. Several inconspicuous members in 1614 became leading figures in the later Jacobean parliaments. They included Sir Thomas Wentworth (the future Earl of Strafford), James Whitelocke, Sir Robert Phelips, and John Eliot.

To these men as well as to their less conspicuous brethren the Addled Parliament taught several valuable lessons. One of these lessons, well learned by the 1620's, was the opposition's need for leadership. The complete failure of the Addled Parliament from any point of view came most immediately from lack of control. Neither the royal officials nor the leading members (scarcely leaders) of the opposition were able to check its turbulent course. While the officials were completely unable to influence the House, the leading members of the opposition found that they could initiate a course of debate but could not control its later stages. Once the Commons began to debate a question, they lost their sense of proportion, becoming more and more violent and ceasing to heed the moderate counsels of experienced members. Ill-feeling and suspicion increased to such an extent under the stimulus of violent and irresponsible conduct that even the opposition leaders themselves quarrelled publicly. Before any opposition to the Crown could become effective, it had to create the internal discipline which would prevent the ill-judged outbursts of 1614.

In the second place, after 1614 the opposition discovered to its sorrow that the King could exist without parliament. Because only three years elapsed between the dissolution of 1611 and the parliament of 1614, its members felt secure in the belief that the government could not function unless parliament met every three or four years. The next seven years, the longest period without a parliament since the Reformation, was a rude shock to those who overestimated the place of parliament in the constitutional structure.

There was little comfort in the obvious fact that parliament met in 1621 only because of the crisis on the Continent. If the Thirty Years War had not involved the King's son-in-law, there was no telling how long parliament might have been postponed. Perhaps simply by summoning it only on rare occasions the King could have left it to atrophy from disuse. With examples all about them of legislative bodies reduced to shadows or relegated to mere tradition, the Commons had a very real fear that the boasted parliament of England might share the same fate.

Another lesson of the Addled Parliament for the opposition arose from the second. If parliament was not to disappear, it would have to play a greater role than the mere obstructionism of 1614. If it could do nothing in reality but reject royal policy and embarrass the Crown, its days were numbered. Blind opposition in parliament was not enough once it became clear that it would not paralyse the government. The King was in the stronger position, for he could gain his ends merely by retaining his position and powers. Fortunately for parliament, in the early Stuart period it was dealing with James I and Charles I. If a Charles II unembarrassed by the religious issue had been on the throne, the Civil War might never have occurred.

After 1614 it was clear that parliament could not maintain a static position. The only alternative to an increase in its power was loss of power. If it contented itself with a negative obstructionism, it would inevitably lose its place in the constitutional scheme. Parliament had no hope of retaining merely the position that it had occupied from 1601 to 1614. If it did not advance, it would certainly regress.

Whatever concept of the late medieval constitution the parliamentarians may have had, they were really advancing into new territory when they tried to expand their powers in the 1620's. If the Crown was not to swallow up all the important functions of parliament, parliament would have to encroach, to some extent at least, on the spheres of royal authority. Of course in such a development two questions would immediately arise. One was the extent of parliamentary encroachment on the royal authority. The other was the machinery through which this control would be exercised.

In both of these fields only a slight advance was made in 1614. Except for finance no area of royal authority was threatened. Here the Commons attacked extra-parliamentary taxation as they had in 1610. But foreign affairs were not touched, and despite Parry's expulsion parliament did not attempt to tamper with the executive. Although there was a hint that taxes should be expended as parliament might direct, even this modest proposal received no conspicuous support. For the opposition the Addled Parliament simply posed the problems without suggesting even tentative solutions.

Chapter XIII

Neither an End nor a Beginning

THE rapid and complete failure of the Addled Parliament struck contemporaries with ominous significance, yet later historians have largely ignored it. The reason is perhaps the negative character of this parliament. The important questions are what it did not do, and why it accomplished nothing.

But in the welter of confusion one important accomplishment of the Addled Parliament was perhaps unrealized even by its members. The uproar raised over the undertakers certainly resulted from no great conspiracy to pack the lower House. Yet it did reflect the contest between the Court and the gentry over the seats no longer under the patronage of the nobility. While the Crown had no intention of electing a compact and stable majority party, it did grope in the direction of succeeding to the patronage of the declining nobility. If it had succeeded, the House of Commons might have declined until it represented no real force in the government. Parliament might have remained, but only in the same status as the innocuous diets of the Continent. Even had it continued to exist, it would not have been a check on royal power, and it would not have been a focal point for public opinion. England might have followed various continental powers on the road to absolutism cloaked by vestigial representative institutions.

But the clamorous attack on the undertakers discredited the Crown's efforts. After 1614 the Crown made no attempt to contest the ascendancy of the gentry in the shires. The middle way of an absolutism disguised behind a parliamentary façade disappeared in 1614. After 1614 two courses remained: either the King must suppress parliament entirely, or he must be prepared to share his power.

But the negativism of the Addled Parliament was more apparent than its accomplishments. While this negativism pervaded the whole parliament, it was most striking in the leadership of the principal officials. With much justice the responsibility for failure fell heavily on them. An examination of the day-to-day proceedings of the House of Commons reveals one striking fact: the leading officials failed because they did not lead. The initiative passed from the Crown because no one of its spokesmen could fill the position of a real leader in the House of Commons.

This failure of leadership was continually apparent. The House of Commons debated inflammatory issues because the officials did not lead it in other directions. When important questions arose or when the interests of the Crown were attacked, the leading officials, especially the privy councillors, were slow to speak and sometimes did not speak at all. Not only were they reluctant to engage in debate, but even when they had ample notice, they made little preparation. Perhaps they might have been excused for lacking an adequate answer for an unexpected attack, but they were equally feeble when they had had sufficient warning.

Worse even than this lack of preparation was their failure to adapt themselves to the changing course of a debate. The arguments of the opposition were often crabbed and illogical, based on a strained interpretation of precedents really inapplicable. Even when other members of the House blasted the arguments of the opposition and reduced them to nonsense, the official leaders would not seize their opportunities. They remained mute in their places while the House passed from one attack on the Crown to another.

While it would appear from a casual survey that the officials were at fault, their failings had deeper causes than themselves. Although they fell down badly in their parliamentary duties, their inadequacies reflected more on their master than on themselves. If the privy councillors acted incompetently in the House of Commons, it must be remembered that the King placed them there. In 1614 the King determined the composition of his council, and he was able to secure seats for his advisers in the lower House.

In choosing his councillors the King laboured under several handicaps largely of his own creation. For one thing, he liked to grant peerages to able officials as rewards for their services. Among the councillors in 1614 he had promoted Stanhope, Knollys, and Wotton to the upper House, so that their services in the Commons were lost to him. When parliament was summoned in 1614, only Caesar, Parry, and Sir John Herbert among the councillors were eligible for election to the Commons. As far as is known, Herbert did not try to secure a seat, possibly because of advancing years. Parry was promptly expelled from the House, leaving Caesar as the only experienced councillor in the Commons.

It is true that Caesar was joined by two new councillors, Sir Ralph Winwood, the principal secretary, and Sir Thomas Lake. But both of them were appointed to the council only a week before parliament met, so they were completely unacquainted with council business. Winwood's case was the more striking of the two. Although he was expected to be the leader of the House of Commons, he had never been a member of parliament before. It was complete folly to suppose that an inexperienced official could fill this position after the difficulties in the parliament of 1604. But Winwood laboured under even greater difficulties. While his long service abroad had given him a good knowledge of foreign affairs, he had lost touch with domestic problems. This difference in experience and outlook proved irritating to both sides.

Winwood was more handicapped than Lake by receiving his appointment to office so shortly before parliament met. Although Winwood was supposed to present the council's programme to parliament, he had no part in drafting the programme and little time to acquaint himself with it. Furthermore, he was overwhelmed by the extra-parliamentary duties of his office. With all these demands on his time plus the necessity of maintaining his position against his rivals at Court, it is no wonder that Winwood often seemed unprepared for the business of the lower House.

Not only was Winwood lacking in experience, but also another key figure in the Commons had scarcely more experience than he. Ranulph Crew, the Speaker, had previously sat only in the parliament of 1597, nearly twenty years before. To expect an inexperienced secretary and an inexperienced Speaker to control a factious House was a case of over-optimism bordering on foolhardiness.

The King's meddling in the affairs of the lower House created still another difficulty. Almost invariably his proposals irritated the Commons even when he was trying to make a conciliatory gesture, as in Parry's case. Probably

Winwood's first request for supply was so poorly timed because he was acting on inflexible orders from the King.

This same incident revealed another aspect of the divergence among royal officials. The very considerable block of officials and courtiers which should have formed a cohesive group in the House was sundered even at the top. On this first occasion when the officials asked for supply, both Caesar and Bacon deviated from Winwood's proposal and advocated other methods of approaching the question. Among the lesser officials and courtiers the disintegration was even more apparent. Although a few were persistent defenders of royal policies, the great majority remained completely silent. Some of them went so far as to become outright opponents of the Court. If the privy councillors and important officials are excluded, only 14 members of the official group spoke in support of the Crown. Of its 141 remaining members, 110 were completely silent, 22 were moderates, and 9 opposed the Court. So the group of Court adherents failed absolutely to form a nucleus around which the Crown could rally its supporters. The opponents of the Court in this group almost equalled its articulate supporters. Motivated by jealousy, pique, and self-esteem as well as by principle, they changed their colours completely. In this connexion it should be remembered that among the four members of the Commons imprisoned after the dissolution, Christopher Neville was the son of a peer, and Sir Walter Chute was carver to the King.

All of these facts about officialdom great and small point unerringly to the main defect in the royal administration. Neither Winwood nor Crew was responsible for his lack of experience or for the collapse of morale among the officials. The services of competent men could not be secured nor the cohesion of the official group maintained because of the weakness at the top. This essential and fundamental weakness was certain to persist until the King took firm control over the government and freed it from the venal and selfish interests which dominated it. This step, however, was one that James would not take. Unless some earth-shaking crisis could bring him to his senses, there was no hope of thoroughgoing reforms.

The opposition on its part suffered from equally glaring defects. Most of its supporters had little acquaintance with the problems facing the Crown. Policies requiring a broad and statesmanlike approach were treated on a parochial basis, and the members of the opposition were so dominated by their own local interests that they ignored the wider problems of the government. In particular they approached financial policy unrealistically, not realizing that as prosperity grew the treasury should share in the increasing wealth of the nation. However hard-headed they were in business, the Commons had not yet learned that good government has a price.

But the worst defect of the opposition was their irresponsibility. This was perhaps inevitable as long as their role was negative. In any case they were able critics of the Crown up to a point. When that point was reached, the opposition reflected in its own way the tendency towards disintegration exhibited by the official group. In both cases the nominal leaders lost control. In the case of the official group loss of control resulted in muteness and desertion. In the case of the opposition it led to extremes of violence and disorder. The official group melted away behind its leaders. The opposition rushed forward pell-mell to overwhelm its leaders and convert the House into a cockpit. Until the opposition had learned internal discipline, it could not hope to gain any lasting victories.

With both sides still incompetent to rule in 1614, it is not surprising that the government limped along for another generation without solving its basic problems. England had developed to the point where it had outgrown the strong monarchy of the Tudors, but nothing had replaced it. Although the personality of the new monarch made the change more abrupt than it otherwise might have been, change was in the air when the seventeenth century dawned.

Unfortunately the sixteenth century had trained no other power to exercise the sovereignty wielded by the Tudor monarchs, nor had it pointed to any solution of the constitutional problem. While Crown and parliament could no longer work in harmony, neither one was capable of assuming the burden of government alone. After the failure of the Addled Parliament the King tried personal rule, foreshadowing the years 1629–40. But another series of parliaments and a second period of personal rule were necessary to bring matters to a head.

The Addled Parliament set problems that it could not solve. It proved beyond any doubt that the Tudor constitution had died with Queen Elizabeth. While the parliament of 1604 might have been regarded as a case of unfortunate incidents between a new King and a tactless parliament, there was no superficial excuse for the failure of the Addled Parliament, and the collapse of the old system was all too evident. The Addled Parliament also indicated that no solution to the constitutional problem was in sight. No stable structure of government would develop before the first of the Stuarts had followed his predecessor to the grave.

Note on Bibliography

THE material available for the study of the Addled Parliament has increased markedly since Gardiner did his great work. Although the *Commons Journals* must always remain the basic source, many supplementary sources have come to light in recent years.

The manuscript sources include the State Papers Domestic, scattered through which there is a wealth of material on all aspects of early Stuart government. The volumes numbered 14/70, 14/74, 14/75, 14/76, 14/77, 14/81, 14/83, 14/90, 14/93, 14/96, and 15/40 were especially useful for this work. Other material was found in State Papers 99/15 and 99/16 (Venice correspondence). The Star Chamber records (St. Ch. 8/293 : 11) contain one election case for 1614.

Two other sources in the Public Record Office were the Spanish and French transcripts (12/34, 12/35, 12/36, and 12/37, and 3/47 and 3/48). These dispatches of Sarmiento and Puysieux throw additional light on the events of 1614. A few of Sarmiento's dispatches are printed in F. Francisco de Jesus, *Narrative of the Spanish Marriage Treaty* (Camden Society, 1869).

In the British Museum the best-known manuscripts on this subject are found in the Cottonian collection. Most of the material is found in Titus B vii, C vi, and F iv. It covers many phases of early Stuart government.

Some important material is found in the Harleian manuscripts. A list of the bills of grace with enlightening notations is in no. 4289. The text of the King's speech of 9 April 1614 is found in no. 6258A, and no. 5176 has information on the opening of parliament in 1614.

In the Lansdowne manuscripts, nos. 486 and 487 are more legible transcripts of the Cottonian F iv material. No. 165 has a list of Jacobean pensions, and no. 222 a list of grants of office, both useful for this work. No. 513 has an extremely important account of the debate in the House of Lords on impositions. This account, which seems not to have been used before, throws considerable light on the most important debate of the session in the upper House.

The Additional Manuscripts have little interesting material. Nos. 11053, 24346, and 34079 throw some light on elections and on the first days of the session. The extracts from the privy council registers in no. 11402 are valuable.

On the whole the manuscripts in the House of Lords are of little use. They consist mainly of drafts of minor bills, mostly private ones, plus the original of the commission dissolving parliament. But the election petition from Norfolk (calendared in *H.M.C. Rept. 4*, appendix, supplemental calendar) is interesting and throws some light on popular opinion and election practices in 1614.

Some materials relating to the Addled Parliament are found in the Bodleian MS. Eng. Hist. c. 286. They are part of the papers of Nathaniel Johnston, a Yorkshire antiquary, who seems to have removed them from Wentworth Woodhouse. There is also a letter relating to this parliament written by Thomas Wentworth on 25 April 1614. It is found in the Sheffield Central Library, Wentworth Woodhouse Papers, Strafford MSS., vol. 34. The Ellesmere papers contain nothing of interest.

The printed sources are really of greater value than the less well-known manuscript sources. Some printed sources, such as the various *Calendars of State Papers* and *The Court and Times of James the First*, have been known for years. *The Letters of John Chamberlain*, a complete edition by N. E. McClure (2 vols., Philadelphia, 1939), supplements the less complete *Court and Times*.

But three new sources on the Addled Parliament have come to light recently. In vol. vii of *Commons Debates for 1621*, edited by Notestein, Relf, and Simpson, there is a diary of events in the House of Commons in 1614 found among the Yelverton manuscripts. A short account by Sir John Holles, a member of this parliament, is printed in *H.M.C. Portland MSS.*, vol. ix. It is taken from his letter book. These two accounts are the only ones known for this parliament besides the *Commons Journals*.

An even more important source is in *H.M.C. Hastings MSS.*, vol. iv. This is an account of considerable length of proceedings in the House of Lords in 1614, probably written by the Earl of Huntingdon. It serves to fill out the scanty record of the *Lords Journals* and is the single most valuable new source.

The Historical Manuscripts Commission's publications have yielded much other useful material. The chief sources were the Trumbull papers (*Downshire*, iv), the Winwood papers (*Buccleuch*, i), and the Montague papers (*Buccleuch*, iii).

Two little-known sources written by members of the Addled Parliament are *The Liber Famelicus of Sir James Whitelocke* and *The Journal of Sir Roger Wilbraham*. The *Interim Report of the Committee on House of Commons Personnel and Politics 1264–1832* has a good account of the compilation of lists of members of the lower House, and its bibliography of borough records is very useful. The numerous collections of individual borough records are, of course, of particular interest for elections and biographical data.

The writings of three important figures in the Addled Parliament are easily available: L. B. Osborn, *The Life, Letters and Writings of John Hoskyns* (New Haven, 1937); L. P. Smith, *The Life and Letters of Sir Henry Wotton* (2 vols., Oxford, 1907); and J. Spedding, *The Letters and Life of Francis Bacon* (7 vols., London, 1868–74).

Among secondary works two of the most helpful have been D. H. Willson, *The Privy Councillors in the House of Commons 1604–1629* (Minneapolis, 1940) and his article 'Summoning and Dissolving Parliament 1603–25', in *The American Historical Review*, xlv. 279–300 (Jan. 1940). His more recent *King James VI and I* (New York, 1956) has filled a gap long felt in this period.

For purposes of comparison there are fortunately three excellent works available: J. E. Neale, *The Elizabethan House of Commons* (London, 1949); D. Brunton and D. H. Pennington, *Members of the Long Parliament* (London, 1954); and M. F. Keeler, *The Long Parliament, 1640–1641: A Biographical Study of its Members* (Philadelphia, 1954).

Other useful secondary sources are the histories of local parliamentary representation, such as the works of Alexander,

Williams, and Wedgwood. Local histories sometimes prove enlightening on elections.

The chief gap in information on this parliament is still in local history. As more local and family records become available to the historian, the election picture will become more complete.

Appendix I

The Privy Council in 1614

*George Abbot, Archbishop of Canterbury. 1611.
*Lord Ellesmere, Lord Chancellor. 1596.
*Earl of Exeter. 1603.
*Earl of Northampton, Lord Keeper of the Privy Seal. 1603.
*Earl of Nottingham, Lord Admiral. c. 1585.
*Earl of Pembroke. 1611.
*Earl of Shrewsbury. 1601.
*Earl of Somerset. 1612.
*Earl of Suffolk, Lord Chamberlain. 1603.
*Earl of Worcester, Master of the Horse. 1601.
*Lord Knollys, Treasurer of the Household. 1596.
*Lord Stanhope, Vice-chamberlain and Treasurer of the Chamber. c. 1596.
*Lord Zouch. c. 1612.

*Duke of Lennox (Scottish title: Earl of Richmond in England). 1603.
Earl of Dunfermline (Scottish title), Lord Chancellor of Scotland. 1609.
Earl of Mar (Scottish title). 1603.
Viscount Fenton (Scottish title). 1610.

†Sir Julius Caesar, Chancellor of the Exchequer. 1607.
Sir Edward Coke, Lord Chief Justice. 4 November 1613.
Sir John Herbert, Second Secretary. 1600.
†Sir Thomas Lake. 29 March 1614.
†Sir Thomas Parry, Chancellor of the Duchy of Lancaster. 1607.
†Sir Ralph Winwood, Principal Secretary of State. 29 March 1614.

* Members of the House of Lords in 1614.
† Members of the House of Commons in 1614.
The dates are those of admission to the Privy Council.

174

Appendix II

The House of Lords in 1614

Lord Chancellor

*Lord Ellesmere (Thomas Egerton, 1540?–1617). Lord Chancellor and a baron 1603. Created Viscount Brackley 1616.

Earls

Cumberland (Francis Clifford, 1559–1641). Succeeded 1605.

Derby (William Stanley, c. 1561–1642). Succeeded 1594.

Dorset (Richard Sackville, 1589–1624). Succeeded 1609.

Essex (Robert Devereux, 1591–1646). Title restored 1604.

*Exeter (Thomas Cecil, 1542–1622). Succeeded as Lord Burghley 1598. Created Earl of Exeter 1605.

Hertford (Edward Seymour, 1539?–1621). Created Earl of Hertford 1559.

Huntingdon (Henry Hastings, 1586–1643). Succeeded 1604.

Montgomery (Philip Herbert, 1584–1650). Created Earl of Montgomery 1605.

*Northampton (Henry Howard, 1540–1614). Created Earl of Northampton 1604. Lord Privy Seal 1608.

*Nottingham (Charles Howard, 1536–1624). Succeeded as Lord Howard of Effingham 1573. Created Earl of Nottingham 1596. Lord Admiral 1585.

*Pembroke (William Herbert, 1580–1630). Succeeded 1601.

*Richmond (Ludovic Stuart, 1574–1624). Succeeded as Duke of Lennox in Scotland 1583. Created Earl of Richmond in England 1613 and Duke of Richmond 1623.

Rutland (Francis Manners, 1578–1632). Succeeded 1612.

Salisbury (William Cecil, 1591–1668). Succeeded 1612.

*Shrewsbury (Gilbert Talbot, 1553–1616). Summoned to Parliament in his father's barony 1588. Succeeded 1590.

* Privy councillors in 1614.

*Somerset (Robert Carr, died 1645). Created Viscount Roches-
  ter 1611 and Earl of Somerset 1613.
Southampton (Henry Wriothesley, 1573–1624). Succeeded
  1581, but attainted 1601. Re-created Earl of Southampton
  1603.
*Suffolk (Thomas Howard, 1561–1626). Created Baron Howard
  de Walden 1597, and Earl of Suffolk 1603. Lord Chamberlain 1603.
Sussex (Robert Radclyffe, c. 1560–1629). Succeeded 1593.
*Worcester (Edward Somerset, 1553–1628). Succeeded 1589.

Viscount Lisle (Robert Sidney, 1563–1626). Created a baron
  1603 and Viscount Lisle 1605.

Barons

Arundell (Thomas Arundell, c. 1560–1639). Created a baron
  1605.
Bergavenny (Edward Neville, c. 1550–1622). Successfully
  claimed the barony 1604.
Carew (George Carew, 1555–1629). Created a baron 1605 and
  Earl of Totnes 1626.
Cavendish (William Cavendish, died 1626). Created a baron
  1605 and Earl of Devonshire 1618.
Chandos (Grey Brydges, 1579?–1621). Succeeded 1602.
Compton (William Compton, c. 1568–1630). Succeeded 1589.
  Created Earl of Northampton 1618.
Dacre (Henry Lennard, 1570–1616). Succeeded mother 1612.
Danvers (Henry Danvers, 1573–1644). Created a baron 1603
  and Earl of Danby 1626.
Darcy and Meinill (John Darcy, 1579?–1635). Succeeded 1602.
Darcy of Chiche (Thomas Darcy, c. 1565–1640). Succeeded
  1581. Created Viscount Colchester 1621 and Earl Rivers
  1626.
De La Warr (Thomas West, 1577–1618). Succeeded 1602.
Denny (Edward Denny, 1569–1637). Created a baron 1604 and
  Earl of Norwich 1626.
Eure (Ralph Eure, 1558–1617). Succeeded 1594.
Gerard (Thomas Gerard, died 1618). Created a baron 1603.

* Privy councillors in 1614.

Grey de Groby (Henry Grey, died 26 July 1614). Created a baron 1603.

Herbert (Henry Somerset, 1577–1646). Eldest son of the Earl of Worcester. Summoned in his father's barony 1604. Succeeded as Earl of Worcester 1628. Created Marquess of Worcester 1643.

Howard de Walden (Theophilus Howard, 1584–1640). Eldest son of the Earl of Suffolk. Summoned in his father's barony 1610. Succeeded as Earl of Suffolk 1626.

Howard of Effingham (William Howard, 1577–1615). Eldest son of the Earl of Nottingham. Summoned in his father's barony 1604. Died before his father.

Hunsdon (John Carey, died 1617). Succeeded 1603.

*Knollys (William Knollys, 1547–1632). Created a baron 1603, Viscount Wallingford 1616, and Earl of Banbury 1626.

Knyvet (Thomas Knyvet, died 1622). Created a baron 1607.

Monteagle (William Parker, 1575–1622). Eldest son of Lord Morley. Created a baron 1605. Succeeded as Lord Morley 1618.

Norris (Francis Norris, 1579–1623). Succeeded 1601. Created Earl of Berkshire 1621.

North (Dudley North, 1581–1666). Succeeded 1600.

Paget (William Paget, 1572–1629). Title restored 1603.

Petre (William Petre, 1575–1637). Succeeded 1613.

Rich (Robert Rich, c. 1560–1619). Succeeded 1581. Created Earl of Warwick 1618.

Russell (Francis Russell, 1593–1641). Succeeded 1613. Succeeded as Earl of Bedford 1627.

St. John (Oliver St. John, died 1618). Succeeded 1596.

Saye and Sele (William Fiennes, 1582–1662). Succeeded 1613. Created Viscount Saye and Sele 1624.

Scrope (Emanuel Scrope, 1584–1630). Succeeded 1609. Created Earl of Sunderland 1627.

Sheffield (Edmund Sheffield, 1564?–1646). Succeeded 1568. Created Earl of Mulgrave 1626.

Spencer (Robert Spencer, died 1627). Created a baron 1603.

Stafford (Edward Stafford, 1573–1625). Succeeded 1603.

* Privy councillor in 1614.

*Stanhope (John Stanhope, 1545?–1621). Created a baron 1605.

Wentworth (Thomas Wentworth, 1591–1667). Succeeded 1593. Created Earl of Cleveland 1626.

Wharton (Philip Wharton, 1555–1625). Succeeded 1572.

Willoughby de Eresby (Robert Bertie, 1572–1642). Succeeded 1601. Created Earl of Lindsey 1626.

Windsor (Thomas Windsor, 1591–1641). Succeeded 1605.

*Wotton (Edward Wotton, 1548–1626). Created a baron 1603.

*Zouch (Edward la Zouch, 1556?–1625). Succeeded 1569.

SPIRITUAL LORDS PRESENT IN 1614

Archbishops

*Canterbury (George Abbot, 1562–1633). Consecrated a bishop 1609. Translated to Canterbury 1611.

York (Tobias Matthew, 1546–1628). Consecrated a bishop 1595. Translated to York 1606.

Bishops

Bath and Wells (James Montague, c. 1568–1618). Consecrated Bishop of Bath and Wells 1608. Translated to Winchester 1616.

Bristol (John Thornborough, 1551–1641). Consecrated a bishop 1593. Translated to Bristol 1603 and to Worcester 1617.

Chester (George Lloyd, 1560–1615). Consecrated a bishop 1600. Translated to Chester 1605.

Chichester (Samuel Harsnett, 1561–1631). Consecrated Bishop of Chichester 1609. Translated to Norwich 1619 and to York 1629.

Coventry and Lichfield (John Overall, 1560–1619). Consecrated Bishop of Coventry and Lichfield 1614. Translated to Norwich 1618.

Durham (William James, 1542–1617). Consecrated Bishop of Durham 1606.

Ely (Launcelot Andrewes, 1555–1626). Consecrated a bishop 1605. Translated to Ely 1609 and to Winchester 1619.

* Privy councillors in 1614.

Exeter (William Cotton, died 1621). Consecrated Bishop of Exeter 1598.

Gloucester (Miles Smith, c. 1568–1624). Consecrated Bishop of Gloucester 1612.

Lincoln (Richard Neile, 1562–1640). Consecrated a bishop 1608. Translated to Lincoln 1614, to Durham 1617, to Winchester 1628, and to York 1632.

Llandaff (Francis Godwin, 1562–1633). Consecrated Bishop of Llandaff 1601. Translated to Hereford 1617.

London (John King, c. 1559–1621). Consecrated Bishop of London 1611.

Oxford (John Bridges, died 1618). Consecrated Bishop of Oxford 1604.

Peterborough (Thomas Dove, 1555–1630). Consecrated Bishop of Peterborough 1601.

Rochester (John Buckeridge, c. 1562–1631). Consecrated Bishop of Rochester 1611. Translated to Ely 1628.

St. Asaph (Richard Parry, 1560–1623). Consecrated Bishop of St. Asaph 1604.

Winchester (Thomas Bilson, 1547–1616). Consecrated a bishop 1596. Translated to Winchester 1597.

Worcester (Henry Parry, 1561–1616). Consecrated a bishop 1607. Translated to Worcester 1610.

PEERS ABSENT IN 1614

Marquess of Winchester (William Paulet, before 1560–1629). Succeeded 1598.

Earls

Arundel (Thomas Howard, 1586–1646). Created an earl 1603. Abroad in 1614.

Bath (William Bourchier, 1557–1623). Succeeded 1561.

Bedford (Edward Russell, 1572–1627). Succeeded 1585.

Kent (Henry Grey, 1541–1615). Succeeded 1573.

Lincoln (Henry Clinton otherwise Fiennes, c. 1542–1616). Succeeded 1585.

Northumberland (Henry Percy, 1564–1632). Succeeded 1585. In the Tower 1605–21.

Oxford (Henry de Vere, 1593–1625). Succeeded 1604. Abroad in 1614.

Barons

Audley (George Tuchet, 1551–1617). Succeeded 1563.

Berkeley (George Berkeley, 1601–58). Succeeded 1613. A minor in 1614.

Clifton (Gervase Clifton, c. 1569–1618). Created a baron 1608.

Clinton (Thomas Clinton otherwise Fiennes, c. 1568–1619). Eldest son of the Earl of Lincoln. Summoned in his father's barony 1610. Succeeded as Earl of Lincoln 1616.

Cromwell (Thomas Cromwell, 1594–1653). Succeeded 1607. A minor in 1614. Created Viscount Lecale 1624 and Earl of Ardglass 1645, both in the Irish peerage.

Dudley (Edward Sutton or Dudley, 1567–1643). Succeeded 1586.

Mordaunt (John Mordaunt, 1599–1644). Succeeded 1609. A minor in 1614. Created Earl of Peterborough 1628.

Sandys (William Sandys, died 1623). Succeeded c. 1560.

Stourton (Edward Stourton, c. 1557–1633). Succeeded 1588.

Vaux (Edward Vaux, 1588–1661). Succeeded 1595.

BISHOPS ABSENT IN 1614

Bangor (Henry Rowlands, 1551–1616). Consecrated Bishop of Bangor 1599.

Carlisle (Henry Robinson, c. 1553–1616). Consecrated Bishop of Carlisle 1598.

Hereford (Robert Bennet, died 1617). Consecrated Bishop of Hereford 1603.

Norwich (John Jegon, 1550–1618). Consecrated Bishop of Norwich 1603.

St. David's (Anthony Rudd, c. 1549–1615). Consecrated Bishop of St. David's 1594.

Salisbury (Henry Cotton, died 1615). Consecrated Bishop of Salisbury 1598.

PEERS RESTORED TO THEIR TITLES BY KING JAMES

Earl of Arundel (Thomas Howard) 1603. Father attainted 1595. Absent in 1614.

Earl of Essex (Robert Devereux) 1604. Father attainted 1601.

Earl of Southampton (Henry Wriothesley) 1603. Attainted 1601.

Lord Paget (William Paget) 1605. Father attainted 1587.

PEERS OWING PROMOTIONS TO KING JAMES

Earl of Dorset (Richard Sackville). Father promoted from baron to earl 1604.

*Earl of Exeter (Thomas Cecil) 1605. Succeeded as Lord Burghley 1598.

*Earl of Richmond (Ludovic Stuart) 1613. Succeeded as Duke of Lennox in Scotland 1583.

*Earl of Suffolk (Thomas Howard) 1603. Created a baron 1597.

ELDEST SONS OF PEERS SUMMONED IN THEIR FATHERS' BARONIES BY KING JAMES

Lord Herbert (Henry Somerset) 1604 (Earl of Worcester).

Lord Howard de Walden (Theophilus Howard) 1610 (Earl of Suffolk).

Lord Howard of Effingham (William Howard) 1604 (Earl of Nottingham).

Lord Clinton (Thomas Clinton otherwise Fiennes) 1610 (Earl of Lincoln). Absent in 1614.

NEW CREATIONS BY KING JAMES
Earls

Montgomery (Philip Herbert) 1605.

*Northampton (Henry Howard) 1604.

Salisbury (William Cecil). Father created a baron 1603, a viscount 1604, and an earl 1605.

*Somerset (Robert Carr). Created a viscount 1611 and an earl 1613.

Viscount Lisle (Robert Sidney). Created a baron 1603 and a viscount 1605.

Barons

*Ellesmere (Thomas Egerton) 1603. (Lord Chancellor.)

Arundell (Thomas Arundell) 1605.

* Privy councillors in 1614.

Carew (George Carew) 1605.
Cavendish (William Cavendish) 1605.
Clifton (Gervase Clifton) 1608. Absent in 1614.
Danvers (Henry Danvers) 1603.
Denny (Edward Denny) 1604.
Gerard (Thomas Gerard) 1603.
Grey de Groby (Henry Grey) 1603.
*Knollys (William Knollys) 1603.
Knyvet (Thomas Knyvet) 1607.
Monteagle (William Parker, the eldest son of Lord Morley) 1605.
Petre (William Petre). Father created a baron 1603.
Russell (Francis Russell). Father created a baron 1603.
Spencer (Robert Spencer) 1603.
*Stanhope (John Stanhope) 1605.
*Wotton (Edward Wotton) 1603.

Attendance in the House of Lords 1614†

Date	Lay Lords	Lords Spiritual	Total	Privy Councillors
Total members:	84	26	110	15
April 5	53	20	73	12
8	50	15	65	12
9	45	11	56	11
11	52	16	68	11
14	44	14	58	9
15	38	15	53	8
16	38	16	54	9
18	35	14	49	9
19	38	14	52	9
May 2	30	15	45	10
3	36	14	50	12
5	42	18	60	11
7	42	16	58	10
9	48	16	64	12
12	43	17	60	10
14	45	18	63	10
16	47	16	63	10

* Privy councillors in 1614.
† Although the House of Lords met on 7 April, there is no record of attendance, so this meeting is omitted from these tables.
The first three columns are inclusive of privy councillors.

Date	Lay Lords	Lords Spiritual	Total	Privy Councillors
19	45	17	62	8
21	52	17	69	11
23	55	16	71	12
24	54	17	71	12
26	51	17	68	12
28	48	18	66	13
30	49	18	67	12
31	50	18	68	13
June 4	43	17	60	11
6	55	19	74	13
7	53	18	71	13

Attendance of individual privy councillors in 1614

	Sessions attended out of 28
Spanish faction	
Earl of Northampton	2
Earl of Nottingham	26
Earl of Suffolk	28
Earl of Somerset	16
Earl of Worcester	19
Lord Knollys	28
Lord Wotton	26
Protestant faction	
Lord Chancellor Ellesmere	28
Archbishop Abbot of Canterbury	28
Earl of Pembroke	27
French faction	
Earl of Richmond (Duke of Lennox)	21
Lord Zouch	23
Others	
Earl of Exeter	2
Earl of Shrewsbury	24
Lord Stanhope	7

Appendix III

Corrections in the List of Members of the House of Commons in 1614[1]

BERKSHIRE

County: Sir Thomas Parry expelled 11 May 1614.
Wallingford: William Reynolds instead of Sir Carey Reynolds.

BUCKINGHAMSHIRE

Chipping Wycombe: Sir Henry Neville chose to sit for Berkshire.

CORNWALL

Lostwithiel: Sir Henry Fann should be Sir Henry Vane.
St. Ives: Sir Anthony Maney also elected for Cirencester.
Saltash: Ralph Carewe should be Ranulph Crew.

CUMBERLAND

County: Sir William Lawson should be Sir Wilfred Lawson.

DORSET

Corfe Castle: Sir Thomas Tracy instead of James Whitelocke.

ESSEX

Harwich: Sir Robert Mansell ('Maunsfielde') chose to sit for Carmarthenshire.

GLOUCESTER

Cirencester: Sir Anthony Maney also elected for St. Ives.

HAMPSHIRE

Stockbridge: the election of Sir Henry Wallop and Sir Walter Cope was voided by the House of Commons 11 May 1614.

[1] The complete list is found in the *Official Return*, i, appendix, pp. xxxvii–xli.

CORRECTIONS IN THE LIST OF MEMBERS, 1614

LANCASHIRE

Liverpool: Edward Wymarke also elected for Peterborough and Newcastle-under-Lyme.

NORTHAMPTONSHIRE

Peterborough: Edward Wymarke also elected for Liverpool and Newcastle-under-Lyme.

NORTHUMBERLAND

County: Sir George Selby elected, but declared ineligible 13 April 1614 because he was sheriff of Durham. Sir William Selby elected in his place 12 May 1614.

NOTTINGHAMSHIRE

East Retford: Sir William Cavendish chose to sit for Derbyshire.

SHROPSHIRE

Ludlow: Robert Berry elected, but declared ineligible 14 April 1614 because he was bailiff of Ludlow. Robert Lloyd elected in his place 11 May 1614.

STAFFORDSHIRE

Lichfield: Sir John Egerton died 27 April 1614. Anthony Dyott elected in his place.

Newcastle-under-Lyme: Edward Wymarke also elected for Liverpool and Peterborough.

SUFFOLK

Bury St. Edmunds: received the right to return two members in 1607, but is omitted entirely from the list.

Ipswich: William Cage in place of Sir Francis Bacon, who chose to sit for Cambridge University.

WARWICKSHIRE

Coventry: Sir Richard Cooke should be Sir Robert Coke.

WILTSHIRE

Hindon: Sir Edwin Sandys chose to sit for Rochester.

APPENDIX III

Hedon: Clement Coke chose to sit for Clitheroe.

County: Sir Richard Bulkeley.

Carmarthen borough: a Mr. Thomas was elected, but the sheriff refused to return him because of a technicality in the writ. Whether or not he ever took his seat is not clear.

Members whose names occur in the records of proceedings, but whose constituencies are not known:
    Mr. Bartlett
    Sir Hugh Beeston
    Sir Carey Reynell
    Mr. Richardson
    Sir Oliver St. John

Appendix IV

The Official Group in the House of Commons

PRIVY COUNCILLORS

Sir Julius Caesar (Middlesex), chancellor of the exchequer 1606:
privy councillor 1607.

Sir Thomas Lake (Middlesex), privy councillor 29 March 1614.

Sir Thomas Parry (Berkshire), chancellor of the duchy of Lancaster and a privy councillor 1607; expelled 11 May 1614.

Sir Ralph Winwood (Buckingham borough), principal secretary
of state and a privy councillor 29 March 1614.

OTHER LEADING OFFICIALS

Sir Francis Bacon (Cambridge University), attorney-general
1613; one of the King's learned counsel.

Ranulph Crew (Saltash), speaker 1614.

Sir George More (Surrey), courtier; chancellor of the Order of
the Garter 1611.

Sir Charles Wilmot (Launceston), Irish privy councillor 1607;
marshal of Ireland 1611.

Sir Henry Wotton (Appleby), ambassador to Venice 1604–12;
half-brother of Lord Wotton, a privy councillor 1602.

Sir Henry Yelverton (Northampton borough), solicitor-general
1613; one of the King's learned counsel.

LEGAL SUPPORTERS OF THE CROWN

Francis Ashley (Dorchester), legal supporter; serjeant 1617.

Robert Barker (Colchester), serjeant 1603.

Leonard Bawtrey (Boston), serjeant July 1614.

Sir John Bennet (Oxford University), chancellor to Queen Anne
c. 1604; a master in chancery 1608.

John Dackombe (Corfe Castle), a master of requests 5 January
1614.

Sir Daniel Dunn (Oxford University), dean of the court of arches 1598; a master in chancery *c.* 1601.

Anthony Dyott (Lichfield), a lawyer in the pay of the Crown 1612.

Henry Finch (St. Albans), serjeant July 1614.

Edward Hendon (Rye), serjeant 1616.

Sir Robert Hitcham (Cambridge borough), attorney-general to Queen Anne 1603.

Sir Francis Leigh (Leicester borough), courtier; a son-in-law of Lord Chancellor Ellesmere; a master of requests 1614.

Sir James Ley (Bath), attorney to the court of wards 1608.

Sir Henry Montague (London), King's serjeant 1611; one of the King's learned counsel.

Francis Moore (Reading), serjeant July 1614.

Edward Mosley (Preston), attorney-general of the duchy of Lancaster by 1614.

George Newman (Canterbury), ecclesiastical lawyer; chancellor of the diocese of Canterbury.

Lewis Prowde (Shrewsbury), justice in North Wales 1611.

Sir Henry Townsend (Ludlow), associate to the chief justice of Chester by 1611.

William Towse (Beverley), serjeant July 1614.

Thomas Trevor (Newport, Cornwall), the prince's solicitor by 1614; one of the King's learned counsel.

Sir Roger Wilbraham (Cheshire), master of requests.

Sir Richard Williamson (Richmond), a master of requests in 1614.

LESSER OFFICIALS

William Beecher (Knaresborough), diplomatic official; auditor of the court of wards 1615.

Henry Binge (Sudbury), keeper of the records of the king's bench 1607.

John Bingley (Chester city), writer of tallies in the exchequer by 1609.

Sir Robert Brett (Dover), gentleman usher at Court; pension 1607; lieutenant of Dover Castle 1614; deputy warden of the Cinque Ports.

Sir Edward Cary (Calne), master of the jewel house by 1614.

Richard Connock (Liskeard), auditor of the Duchy of Cornwall 1609.

Sir William Cook (Gloucestershire), clerk of the liveries 1610.

Sir Walter Cope (Stockbridge), master of the wards 1613; election voided 11 May 1614.

Sir William Cornwallis (Orford), treasurer of Prince Henry's household 1609–12.

Francis Crane (Penryn), clerk of parliament 1606; secretary to Prince Charles.

Sir Lionel Cranfield (Hythe), surveyor-general of the customs 1613.

Sir Roger Dallison (Malmesbury), lieutenant of the ordnance c. 1607.

Edmund Doubleday (Westminster), warden of the mint.

Thomas Fanshawe (Lancaster borough), surveyor-general and auditor of the Duchy of Lancaster by 1610.

William Fanshawe (Lancaster borough), auditor of the Duchy of Lancaster; son of Thomas Fanshawe.

Sir Miles Fleetwood (Huntingdon borough), receiver of the court of wards 1610.

John Griffith (Portsmouth), secretary and assistant to the lord warden of the Cinque Ports by 1612.

Sir Robert Johnson (Monmouth borough), an officer of the ordnance.

Sir Robert Mansell (Carmarthenshire), treasurer of the navy 1604.

Sir Humphrey May (Westminster), groom of the king's privy chamber 1604.

Sir Thomas Monson (Cricklade), master falconer 1605; keeper of the naval arsenal in the Tower 1612.

Robert Naunton (Camelford), clerk in the secretary's office 1611.

William Pitt (Wareham), a minor official.

William Ravenscroft (Old Sarum), clerk of the petty bag 1598.

Sir George Rivers (East Grinstead), in the alienation office.

Thomas Russell (Truro), a minor official by 1611.

Sir Nicholas Smith (St. Mawes), receiver-general for Middlesex, Herts., Essex, and London.

Sir Thomas Smyth (Sandwich), receiver of the Duchy of Cornwall.

John Suckling (Reigate), a minor official.

Simon Thelwall (Denbighshire), proctor of the court of arches.

Sir John Trevor (Bletchingley), surveyor of royal ships 1598.

Thomas Watson (Rye), teller in the exchequer 1605.

CLOSE RELATIVES OF OFFICIALS

Francis Beale (Northampton borough), brother-in-law of Sir Henry Yelverton, solicitor-general and M.P. 1614.

Sir Charles Caesar (Weymouth and Melcombe Regis), son of Sir Julius Caesar, a privy councillor and M.P. 1614.

Sir Philip Cary (Woodstock), son of Sir Edward Cary, master of the jewel house and M.P. 1614.

Sir Richard Cecil (Stamford), second son of the Earl of Exeter, a privy councillor.

Thomas Chettle (Worcester city), son-in-law of one Hanbury, an auditor to King James.

Clement Cook (Clitheroe) and Sir Robert Coke (Coventry), sons of Sir Edward Coke, lord chief justice.

Henry Croke (Shaftesbury) and Sir John Croke (Oxfordshire), sons of Sir John Croke, a justice of the king's bench.

John Dunn (Taunton), son of Sir Daniel Dunn, a master in chancery.

Philip Fleming (Lymington) and Sir Thomas Fleming (Southampton borough), sons of Sir Thomas Fleming, lord chief justice 1607–13.

Sir Robert Knollys (Abingdon), a brother of Lord Knollys, a privy councillor.

Robert Knollys (Reading), nephew of Lord Knollys.

Henry Ley (Westbury), son of Sir James Ley, attorney to the court of wards.

Matthew Ley (Westbury), brother of Sir James Ley.

Edward Littleton (Bishop's Castle), son of the chief justice of North Wales.

Sir Thomas Mansell (Glamorganshire), brother of Sir Robert Mansell, treasurer of the navy.

Sir Edward Montague (Northamptonshire), Sidney Montague

(Wells), and Sir Walter Montague (Monmouthshire), brothers of Sir Henry Montague, the King's serjeant.

Sir Robert Phelips (Saltash), son of Sir Edward Phelips, master of the rolls.

Robert Ravenscroft (Flintshire), son of William Ravenscroft, clerk of the petty bag and M.P. 1614.

Sir Henry Savile (Aldborough), a son of Sir John Savile, a baron of the exchequer 1598–1607.

Sir Richard Smyth (Hythe), brother of Sir Thomas Smyth, receiver of the Duchy of Cornwall and M.P. 1614.

Sir William Tate (Northamptonshire), son-in-law of Lord Zouch, a privy councillor.

COURTIERS AND PETTY OFFICIALS

Sir John Ashley (Oxford city), courtier; pension 1608; reversion of the deputy mastership of the revels 1612.

Sir William Bampfield (Bridport), captain of Sandsfoot Castle c. 1612.

Sir Edward Barrett (Whitchurch), courtier.

Sir Hugh Beeston (constituency not known), receiver-general in Cheshire, Flint, and Caernarvonshire 1604.

Sir John Brooke (Gatton), pension 1611.

Sir William Button (Morpeth), by 1614 in attendance on foreign ambassadors and receiving a pension.

William Byng (Winchelsea), captain of Deal Castle by 1608.

Sir Henry Carey (Hertfordshire), courtier; a son of Lord Hunsdon.

Sir William Cavendish (Derbyshire), courtier; a son of Lord Cavendish.

Sir Walter Chute (East Retford), carver to the King by 1614.

Ralph Clare (Droitwich), courtier; in Prince Henry's service c. 1606–12; in royal service continuously after c. 1606.

Sir Oliver Cromwell (Huntingdonshire), gentleman of the privy chamber to the Queen by 20 May 1614.

Henry Dade (Dunwich), courtier.

Sir John Danvers (Montgomery borough), pension by 1614; a brother of Lord Danvers.

Sir John Dormer (Aylesbury), royal huntsman and falconer by 1614.

Sir John Egerton (Lichfield), courtier; pension 1610; died 27 April 1614.

Sir George Fane (Dover), temporary lieutenant of Dover Castle.

Philip Gawdy (Dunwich), courtier.

Sir Thomas Gerrard (Lancashire), gentleman of the privy chamber to the Queen by 1614.

Thomas Gibbs (Stafford borough), courtier.

Robert Hatton (Queenborough), courtier; steward of the Archbishop of Canterbury.

Arnold Herbert (Morpeth), pension 1611.

Sir Edward Hoby (Rochester), courtier; gentleman of the privy chamber to King James.

Sir Thomas Posthumous Hoby (Ripon), courtier; several posts of honour.

Sir Gilbert Hoghton (Clitheroe), courtier; carver to the King c. 1614.

Sir Jerome Horsey (Bossiney), a receiver of the King's lands for life c. 1604.

Sir Charles Howard, sr. (Shoreham), courtier; pension by 1614; second son of the Earl of Nottingham, a privy councillor.

Sir Charles Howard, jr. (Bletchingley), courtier; a nephew of the Earl of Nottingham.

Sir Edward Howard (Reigate), courtier; King's cupbearer 1604; a son of the Earl of Nottingham.

Henry Howard (Derbyshire), courtier; third son of the Earl of Suffolk.

Sir Thomas Howard (Wiltshire), courtier; master of the Prince's horse by 1614; a son of the Earl of Suffolk.

Sir Arthur Ingram (Romney), the moneyed man at court; a secretary of the council of the north 1612; pension by 1614.

Sir Thomas Jermyn (Suffolk), courtier and perennial office-seeker.

James Kerton (Ludgershall), pension by 1614.

Sir Robert Killigrew (Helston), pension by 1614; a favourite of Somerset.

Edward Leech (Lostwithiel), tin assayer in Cornwall and Devon 4 March 1614.

Sir John Leeds (Bramber), courtier.

Robert Lloyd (Ludlow), sewer to the Queen.

George Marshall (Boroughbridge), one of the King's equerries in 1612.

Sir William Maynard (Chippenham), courtier.

Giles Mompesson (Great Bedwin), courtier.

Sir Robert More (Guildford), one of the gentlemen pensioners; son of Sir George More, chancellor of the order of the Garter and M.P. 1614.

Meredith Morgan (Berwick-on-Tweed), a minor treasury official.

Roger Palmer (Queenborough), cupbearer to Prince Charles before 25 July 1614.

Sir Thomas Penruddock (Cumberland), a sewer to the King c. 1614.

Sir Carey Reynell (constituency unknown), courtier.

Sir George Reynell (Grantham), marshal of the king's bench.

Sir Henry Rich (Leicester borough), a favourite of King James; gentleman of the bedchamber to Prince Charles; second son of Lord Rich.

Sir Thomas Roe (Tamworth), courtier.

Sir Miles Sandys (Cambridge University), courtier.

Sir William Selby (Northumberland), pension by 1614.

Sir Edward Seymour (Lyme Regis), courtier.

Henry Spiller (Arundel), courtier; official receiving payments from recusants by 1611.

Sir William Strode (Plymouth), courtier; royal surveyor by 1614.

Sir Thomas Tracy (Corfe Castle), a farmer of customs 1612.

Sir William Twisden (Thetford), gentleman usher of the privy chamber.

Sir William Uvedale (Hampshire), a gentleman of the privy chamber to the Queen by 1615.

Sir Henry Vane (Lostwithiel), courtier; sewer to the King c. 1614.

Sir Thomas Vavasor (Horsham), knight marshal of the household 1612.

Sir Thomas Walsingham (Kent), courtier; chief keeper of the Queen's wardrobe *c*. 1604.

Sir Thomas Walsingham, jr. (Poole), courtier.

Sir Richard Weston (Essex), minor official since 1604.

Sir William Woodhouse (Aldeburgh), pension by 1614.

Edward Wymarke (Liverpool, Peterborough, and Newcastle-under-Lyme), courtier.

Richard Wynn (Caernarvonshire), courtier; groom of the chamber to Prince Charles.

OTHER ROYAL SUPPORTERS

Sir Francis Goodwin (Buckinghamshire), elected at Buckingham borough 1606 with council support.

Sir William Killigrew (Penryn), chamberlain of the exchequer 1605–6; father of Sir Robert Killigrew, a favourite of Somerset.

Robert Needham (Newcastle-under-Lyme), son of a courtier.

Sir Henry Neville (Berkshire and Chipping Wycombe), candidate for the secretaryship 1612–14.

Sir Henry Wallop (Stockbridge), owed his election to the council; election voided 11 May 1614.

Robert Wolverston (Cardigan borough), received favours from the King in the autumn of 1614 for his services in parliament.

Appendix V

Connexions of the Peerage in the House of Commons

ELDEST SONS OF PEERS

Sir Mervyn Audley (Dorset), only son of Lord Audley; succeeded as Lord Audley and Earl of Castlehaven (Irish peerage) 1617.

Sir Henry Carey (Hertfordshire), eldest son of Lord Hunsdon; succeeded 1617; later Viscount Rochfort and Earl of Dover.

Henry, Lord Clifford (Westmorland), eldest son of the Earl of Cumberland; succeeded 1641; Baron Clifford 1628; married a daughter of the Earl of Salisbury 1610.

Sir Robert Rich (Essex), eldest son of Lord Rich, who was created Earl of Warwick 1618; succeeded 1619.

Sir Oliver St. John (constituency unknown), eldest son of Lord St. John; succeeded 1618; later Earl of Bolingbroke.

Sir Robert Sidney (Wilton), eldest son of Viscount Lisle, who was created Earl of Leicester 1618; succeeded 1626.

Sir Thomas Wharton (Westmorland), eldest son of Lord Wharton; died before his father.

IMMEDIATE FAMILIES OF PEERS

Sir Peregrine Bertie (Lincolnshire), brother of Lord Willoughby de Eresby; his mother was a daughter of the Earl of Oxford.

Sir William Cavendish (Derbyshire), second son of Lord Cavendish, who was created Earl of Devonshire in 1618; succeeded his father in 1626.

Sir Richard Cecil (Stamford), second son of the Earl of Exeter.

Sir John Danvers (Montgomery borough), a brother of Lord Danvers, who became Earl of Danby in 1626.

Walter Devereux (Pembroke borough), a son of the Earl of Essex.

O 2

Sir Francis Fane (Maidstone), mother was the only daughter and heiress of Lord Bergavenny; in 1604 she was restored to the title of Baroness Le Despencer; Sir Francis Fane became Earl of Westmorland in 1624.

Sir Henry Grey (Bedfordshire), nephew of the Earl of Kent; his father became Earl of Kent in 1615; succeeded in 1623.

George Hastings (Leicestershire), brother of the Earl of Huntingdon.

Sir Charles Howard, sr. (Shoreham) and Sir Edward Howard (Reigate), younger sons of the Earl of Nottingham.

Henry Howard (Derbyshire) and Sir Thomas Howard (Wiltshire), younger sons of the Earl of Suffolk.

Sir Robert Knollys (Abingdon), a brother of Lord Knollys, who became Viscount Wallingford in 1616 and Earl of Banbury in 1626.

Sampson Lennard (Sussex), his wife who died in 1612 became Baroness Dacre in 1594; his son succeeded as Baron Dacre in 1612.

Sir George Manners (Lincolnshire), brother of the Earl of Rutland; succeeded 1632.

Christopher Neville (Lewes), second son of Lord Bergavenny.

Sir Henry Rich (Leicester borough), second son of Lord Rich, who was created Earl of Warwick in 1618; Sir Henry Rich was created Baron Kensington in 1623 and Earl of Holland in 1624.

Sir Alexander St. John (Bedford borough) and Rowland St. John (Higham Ferrers), younger sons of Lord St. John.

William Spencer (Brackley), second son of Lord Spencer; succeeded his father 1627; a son-in-law of the Earl of Southampton.

Sir Henry Wotton (Appleby), half-brother of Lord Wotton.

OTHER CLOSE CONNEXIONS OF THE PEERAGE IN THE HOUSE OF COMMONS

Sir Thomas Cheke (Newport, Cornwall), son-in-law of Lord Rich.

Sir Henry Glemham (Aldeburgh), son-in-law of the Earl of Dorset.

Sir Cuthbert Halsall (Lancashire), wife a natural daughter of the Earl of Derby.

Sir John Holles (Nottinghamshire), grandson of Lord Sheffield; Holles was created a baron in 1616 and Earl of Clare in 1624.

Sir Charles Howard, jr. (Bletchingley), a nephew of the Earl of Nottingham.

Robert Knollys (Reading), a nephew of Lord Knollys.

Sir Francis Leigh (Leicester borough), a son-in-law of Lord Chancellor Ellesmere.

John Poulett (Somerset), grandson of Lord Norris; Poulett was created a baron in 1627.

Nathaniel Rich (Totnes), father an illegitimate son of Lord Rich.

Sir William Tate (Northamptonshire), son-in-law of Lord Zouch.

CLOSE CONNEXIONS OF THE BISHOPS IN THE HOUSE OF COMMONS

Sir Thomas Bilson (Winchester), a son of the Bishop of Winchester.

George Cotton (Camelford), younger brother of the Bishop of Exeter.

Sir Edward Montague (Northamptonshire), Sir Henry Montague (London), Sidney Montague (Wells), and Sir Walter Montague (Monmouthshire), brothers of the Bishop of Bath and Wells.

Appendix VI

Abbreviated Genealogy of the Howard Family

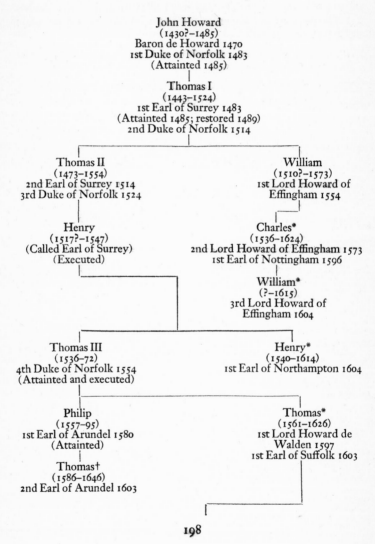

John Howard
(1430?-1485)
Baron de Howard 1470
1st Duke of Norfolk 1483
(Attainted 1485)

Thomas I
(1443-1524)
1st Earl of Surrey 1483
(Attainted 1485; restored 1489)
2nd Duke of Norfolk 1514

Thomas II
(1473-1554)
2nd Earl of Surrey 1514
3rd Duke of Norfolk 1524

William
(1510?-1573)
1st Lord Howard of
Effingham 1554

Henry
(1517?-1547)
(Called Earl of Surrey)
(Executed)

Charles*
(1536-1624)
2nd Lord Howard of Effingham 1573
1st Earl of Nottingham 1596

William*
(?-1615)
3rd Lord Howard of
Effingham 1604

Thomas III
(1536-72)
4th Duke of Norfolk 1554
(Attainted and executed)

Henry*
(1540-1614)
1st Earl of Northampton 1604

Philip
(1557-95)
1st Earl of Arundel 1580
(Attainted)

Thomas†
(1586-1646)
2nd Earl of Arundel 1603

Thomas*
(1561-1626)
1st Lord Howard de
Walden 1597
1st Earl of Suffolk 1603

198

Theophilus*	Elizabeth	Frances
(1584–1640)	m. Lord Knollys*	m. Earl of
2nd Lord Howard	1605	Somerset*
de Walden 1610		1613

* Members of the House of Lords in 1614. Henry, Earl of Northampton, died 15 June 1614, eight days after the Addled Parliament was dissolved.

† Thomas, Earl of Arundel, was a peer in 1614, but he was abroad and never took his seat in the Addled Parliament.

Appendix VII

Lists of Bills drawn up by the Privy Council[1]

*Bills to be drawn by his Majesty's most gracious direction
for the good and comfort of his people upon certain of the
propositions exhibited to his Majesty, and to be offered to
the Parliament*

1. An act for the passing the accounts of Sheriffs, Escheators, Collectors of Subsidies, Tenths, Fifteenths and Aids, without charge or delay.
2. An act for the better avoiding secret offices and inquisitions to be taken on his Majesty's behalf to the prejudice of his subjects.
3. An act giving authority to certain Commissioners to review the state of penal laws, to the end that such as are obsolete and snaring may be repealed, and such as are fit to continue and concern one matter may be reduced respectively into one clear form of law.
4. An act for the safeguard and relief of the King's tenants and farmers in case of forfeiture for non-payment of rent.

*Bills to be drawn by his Majesty's most gracious direction
for the good and comfort of his people, upon certain other
of the propositions exhibited to his Majesty, to be ready if
they be sued for by his Commons*

1. An act for the ordering of the respect of homage to be with less charge and trouble to his Majesty's subjects.
2. An act for the avoiding of the trouble and charge of the King's subjects in the pleadings of the Exchequer in case of alienation by the King's tenants.
3. An act for the admitting of the King's subjects to plead the general issue and to continue their possession in certain

---

[1] These lists are printed in Spedding, *Letters and Life of Bacon*, v. 14–18.

cases upon informations of intrusion exhibited against them.

4. An act for the repeal of a branch of the statute of 34. H. 8. concerning the alteration of laws in Wales without Parliament.

Here the Cottonian manuscript ends, but the Harleian manuscript contains the following in addition:

9. An act against the long continuance of Liveries, and unnecessary bringing in of evidence into the Court of Wards.
10. An act against the vexation of his Majesty's subjects by the assigning of debts unto the Crown.
11. An act for making the estates of attainted persons liable for the payment of their just and true debts.
Further remembrances by his Majesty.
Touching carts taking.
Touching assert lands.
Touching a liberal pardon.

Bills to be drawn by his Majesty's most gracious direction for the general good of the commonwealth, upon other heads besides those that were propounded

1. An act against extortion, and for declaring the just and ancient fees of Courts.
2. An act for the limitation of [the] number of attorneys in the King's Courts.
3. An act against the receivers and maintainers of pirates.
4. An act for the repressing of duels and challenges and the trial of such duels as shall be performed beyond the seas.
5. An act against the bringing in and disposing of seditious books concerning the Pope's authority.

In the margin opposite these last five titles is written 'Civil Policy'. The next four, though marked as a separate class by the recommencement of the numbers, are not included under any general description.

1. An act against (qu. for?) the restraint of building in or near London, and against inmates and dividing of tenements.
2. An act against the intolerable waste and consumption of gold and silver in unnecessary vanities.
3. An act for the breeding and preserving of timber and woods.
4. An act for the supply of the laws concerning depopulation and tillage.

Memorial of secret bills

1. An act for the naturalizing of the Count Palatine and issues between him and the Lady Elizabeth.
2. An act for the better administration of justice and for the declaration and limitation of the jurisdiction of Courts.
3. An act for the beautifying and better government of the city of London, and the suburbs of the same.
4. An act for the suppressing and supply of Boroughs of Parliament according to the present state of the towns of this realm.
5. An act for the better proceeding in the plantation of Ireland.
6. An act for the increase of the wealth of this realm by fishing with busses.
7. An act for a more perfect constitution for the uttering of cloths dressed and undressed.
8. An act for the declaration and conformation of the reasonable liberties of corporations.
9. An act against usury.
10. An act concerning a more certain order in granting letters of administration.

Other Bills to be propounded, not yet consulted upon

1. An act for the moderating of excessive prices of victuals and other commodities.
2. An act for the better policy and government of strangers inhabiting.
3. An act against deceit in weights and measures.

4. An act for the suppressing of certain liberties and exempted places.
5. An act for the better plantation of Virginia and supply thereof.
6. An act to limit the fees of Serjeants, Counsellors at Law, and their clerks.
7. An act to take away the clause of the statute that doth restrain the bringing in of barrelled fish, whereupon a monopoly is founded having a *non obstante*.
8. An act to give the fourth part of the penalties of alehouses and innholders to those that will inform.
9. An act [that] there may be burgesses and knights for the County Palatine of Durham.
10. An act to make a haven at Astworth in the County of Devon.
11. An act to punish abuses upon the Sabbath day.
12. An act for the naturalising of the two daughters of Sir Horatio Vere.
13. An act for the naturalising of Elizabeth Meere.
14. An act to confirm a decree made in Chancery to confirm the inheritance of Sir Thomas Windham, knt., against a grant made to the late Q. Elizabeth and Burtram.
15. An act to restrain Brewers and Alehouse keepers to be justices within any corporation.
16. An act to confirm a decree of customs made between Henry Jernegam and his farmers.
17. An act to enable Sir William Sandes to make his wife an annuity of the manor of Motford against the Lord Sandes and against the heir of the said William Sandes.
18. An act for the selling of certain lands of Sir William Forth in Suff.
19. An act to reform abuses in making brick and tyle.
20. An act for the preserving of the records of the sessions of the Peace.
21. An act to reform deceit in dyeing silk.
22. An act to enable Sir Warwick Heale to make leases of his lands for three lives.
23. An act for the establishing of the hospital appointed by the will of the Earl of Dorset.

24. An act to enable Dame Jane Skinner to have her dower of Castle Camps and other manors.
25. An act to enable William Fletcher of Fleethall in Sussex to sell certain lands.
26. An act to reverse a decree in Chancery for Sir Rowland Lacye.
27. An act to avoid fees exacted by Customers, Controllers, their clerks and other officers, and that merchants may pass away their goods after the custom compounded for.
[28.] An act for to limit a time for the beginning of suits.

Index

Abbot, George, Archbishop of Canterbury, 25, 64, 65, 118, 122, 128, 131, 145, 154.
Abingdon, 49.
Aldborough, 46.
Alford, Edward, 85, 103, 124, 129, 130, 159.
Andrewes, Launcelot, Bishop of Ely, 154.
Arundel, Earl of (Thomas Howard), 1586–1646, 47–48, 63.
Arundell, Thomas, Lord, 33.
Ashley, Francis, 50, 59, 105, 137, 144.
Ashley, Sir John, 49.
Attorney-General, attack on, 85–87, 89–90.
Audley, Lord (George Tuchet), 38, 123.
Audley, Sir Mervyn, 38, 123.

Bacon, Sir Francis, Attorney-General: favours calling parliament, 17–18, 154; plans for managing parliament, 18–23, 28, 69; influence on King's speeches, 71–73, 82–83; election to Commons, 39–40, 50; estimate of new members, 55; eligibility to sit in Commons, 85–88; and supply, 92–93, 94, 112, 167; on undertakers, 70–71, 73, 98–99; introduces bills of grace, 97; defends Parry, 102; and impositions, 111; mentioned, 59, 67.
Baronets, 10, 26.
Bawtrey, Leonard, 101, 111, 148.
Beale, Francis, 50.
Bedingfield, Sir Henry, 34–35.
Beecher, William, 46.
Benevolence, 150–2.
Bennet, Sir John, 39.
Bennet, Robert, Bishop of Hereford, 63.
Bergavenny, Lord, 137.
Berkeley, Sir Maurice, 13, 33, 91, 130, 144.

Berkshire, 31.
Bertie, Sir Peregrine, 34, 38.
Bertie, Robert, see Lord Willoughby de Eresby.
Bills of Grace, 69, 72, 82, 88–89, 90, 92, 93, 95, 97, 137, 151.
Bilson, Thomas, Bishop of Winchester, 35, 63, 122, 131.
Binge, Henry, 46.
Bishops, 7, 65, 79, 150, 152.
Bishop's Castle, 47.
Bletchingley, 47.
Boroughbridge, 46.
Bossiney, 48.
Brakin, Francis, 43.
Bramber, 47.
Breton, Henry, 105.
Bristol, 90.
Brooke, Christopher, 19, 59, 95, 124.
Brooke, Sir John, 49.
Brown, Sir William, 50.
Brydges, Grey, see Lord Chandos.
Buckinghamshire, 31.

Caernarvonshire, 32.
Caesar, Sir Julius, 25, 31, 59, 75, 79, 83–84, 92, 94, 137, 154, 165, 167.
Cage, Sir John, 38.
Calvinism, 5.
Cambridge, 43.
Cambridge University, 39, 50, 57, 58.
Cambridgeshire, 38.
Camelford, 48.
Cardiff, 49.
Cardigan, 148.
Carey, Sir Henry, 32, 38.
Carey, John, see Lord Hunsdon.
Carleton, Sir Dudley, 26.
Carmarthen, 52.
Carmarthenshire, 32, 52.
Carr, Robert, see Earl of Somerset.
Cavendish, William, Lord, 32, 38.
Cavendish, Sir William, 32, 38.
Cecil, Robert, see 1st Earl of Salisbury.

205

INDEX

Cecil, Thomas, *see* Earl of Exeter.

Cecil, William, *see* 2nd Earl of Salisbury.

Chamberlain, John, 12, 24, 26, 78, 83, 89, 153.

Chandos, Lord, 121, 131.

Charles I, 34, 78, 116, 161.

Charles II, 161.

Cheshire, 32.

Chichley, Sir Thomas, 38.

Church of England, 2, 5, 7, 17, 91, 109–10, 124.

Chute, Sir Walter, 134, 146–7, 167.

Civil War, 1, 34, 35, 161.

Clifford, Francis, *see* Earl of Cumberland.

Clifford, Henry, Lord, 38.

Clifton, Gervase, Lord, 64.

Clinton otherwise Fiennes, Henry, *see* Earl of Lincoln.

Clinton, Lord (Thomas Clinton otherwise Fiennes), 63, 64.

Clitheroe, 46.

Coke, Clement, 45.

Coke, Sir Edward, 45, 48, 50, 120–1, 150, 154.

Coke, Sir Robert, 50.

Cooke, Sir William, 32.

Cope, Sir Anthony, 32, 37.

Cope, Sir Walter, 31, 45.

Cope, Sir William, 130.

Corbett, Dr., 39–40.

Corfe Castle, 50.

Cornwall, 48.

Cornwallis, Sir Charles, 23, 140, 146.

Cotton, George, 48.

Cotton, Henry, Bishop of Salisbury, 63.

Cotton, Sir John, 38.

Cotton, William, Bishop of Exeter, 48, 63.

Count Palatine, 26, 69, 71–72, 81, 82, 90, 95, 145, 155, 158.

Coventry, 50.

Cranfield, Lionel, 47, 152.

Crew, Ranulph, 42, 48, 59, 83–84, 166, 167.

Crew, Thomas, 93.

Croft, Sir Herbert, 33, 37, 60, 86, 95, 144.

Croke, Henry, 48.

Croke, Sir John, 32, 37.

Crompton, Sir John, 105.

Cromwell, Sir Oliver, 32.

Cromwell, Oliver, 32.

Cumberland, 32.

Cumberland, Earl of (Francis Clifford), 38.

Cutts, Sir John, jr., 38.

Dackome, John, 50.

Dacre, Lord (Henry Lennard), 38.

Dade, Henry, 48.

Danvers, Henry, Lord, 120.

Darcy, Sir Francis, 31.

Dartmouth, 51.

De la Warr, Lord (Thomas West), 119.

Denbighshire, 42.

Derbyshire, 32, 38.

Devereux, Robert, *see* Earl of Essex.

Devizes, 49.

Digby, Sir John, 139.

Digges, Sir Dudley, 19, 31, 59, 95, 98, 111, 115, 124, 125, 132, 159.

Divine Right of Kings, 5, 7.

Dorchester, 50.

Dorset, 38.

Dorset, Earl of (Richard Sackville), 63, 119.

Dove, Thomas, Bishop of Peterborough, 46, 63.

Dover, 47.

Downton, 49.

Duncombe, Edward, 85, 135.

Dunfermline, Earl of, 25, 49.

Dunn, Sir Daniel, 39.

Dunn, John, 50.

Dunwich, 48.

Duport, Dr., 39–41.

Durham, 37.

Dutch Republic, 6, 23, 75, 91.

East Grinstead, 46.

East Looe, 48.

Edmondes, Sir Thomas, 23.

Edward VI, 62.

Egerton, Thomas, *see* Lord Ellesmere.

Elections, 15, 20–21, 22, 70, 81, 88, 94, 163–4.

Elector Palatine, *see* Count Palatine.

206

Elizabeth I, 3, 4, 7, 8, 50, 169.
Elizabeth, Princess, 26, 81, 90, 155, 158.
Eliot, John, 160.
Ellesmere, Lord (Thomas Egerton), Lord Chancellor: supports Protestant faction in council, 25, 64, 65; and elections to Addled Parliament, 43, 50; and impositions, 118, 119, 121, 122, 154; defends Neile, 129; and dissolution, 141, 143, 145; mentioned, 84, 148.
Essex, 31, 38.
Essex, 2nd Earl of (Robert Devereux), 11, 75.
Essex, 3rd Earl of (Robert Devereux), 24, 63.
Exeter, Earl of (Thomas Cecil), 50, 63, 154.

Fanshawe, Thomas, 45.
Fanshawe, William, 45, 102.
Felton, Henry, 44.
Fenton, Viscount, 25, 154.
Fiennes, William, see Lord Saye and Sele.
Finance: problems, 7; in Parliament of 1604, 8; King's penury, 22, 26–28; attempts to find extra-parliamentary revenue, 10, 26–27, 150–2, 162; improvement in, 152–3.
Finch, Henry, 50, 148.
France, 11, 23, 25, 90, 114–15.
French Company, 90–91, 95.
Fuller, Nicholas, 41, 59, 92, 94–95, 98, 125, 126, 130, 138, 159.

Gatton, 49.
Gawdy, Philip, 48.
Gerrard, Sir Thomas, 32, 45.
Gibbs, Thomas, 105.
Gifford, Sir Richard, 45.
Giles, Sir Edward, 146.
Glanville, John, 129.
Gloucestershire, 32.
Godwin, Francis, Bishop of Llandaff, 63.
Gondomar, Count, see Don Diego Sarmiento.
Gooch, Dr., 39–40.
Goodwin, Sir Francis, 31.

Gray, Sir Ralph, 37.
Great contract, 8, 11, 19.
Grievances, 82, 88, 89, 144.
Griffith, John, 47.
Gunpowder Plot, 8, 97–98.

Hakewill, William, 86, 95, 125, 159.
Hampshire, 35–36, 53.
Harvey, Francis, 43–44.
Haslemere, 49.
Hastings, 47.
Hastings, George, 43–44.
Hastings, Henry, see Earl of Huntingdon.
Hatton, Lady, 50, 53.
Helston, 48, 51.
Hendon, Edward, 47.
Henry VII, 2, 3, 62.
Henry VIII, 2, 62, 63.
Henry, Prince of Wales, 11, 25–26, 33, 105.
Henry IV of France, 116, 123, 147.
Herbert, Lord (Henry Somerset), 63.
Herbert, Sir John, 8, 23, 56, 75, 165.
Herbert, Philip, see Earl of Montgomery.
Herbert, William, see Earl of Pembroke.
Herbert, Sir William, 105–6, 108.
Hereford, 147.
Herefordshire, 32, 33, 37.
Hericke, Sir William, 43–44.
Hertford, Earl of (Edward Seymour), 33, 150.
Hertfordshire, 32, 38.
Higham Ferrers, 46.
Hitcham, Sir Robert, 43, 51, 148.
Hitchcock, Thomas, 47, 111.
Hoby, Sir Edward, 42, 130.
Hoby, Sir Thomas Posthumous, 46.
Hoghton, Sir Gilbert, 46.
Holles, Sir John, 19, 23, 32–33, 37, 89.
Horsey, Sir Jerome, 85, 130.
Horsham, 47.
Hoskyns, John: attacks established church, 91, 124; and supply, 93, 95, 144; and undertakers, 98; linked with Earl of Northampton, 124–5, 145; attacks Neile, 124–5;

Hoskyns, John (*cont.*)
  attacks Scots, 138, 139, 140, 142–3;
  imprisoned, 146–7; mentioned, 59.
Howard, Charles, *see* Earl of Nottingham.
Howard, Sir Charles, jr., 47.
Howard, Sir Edward, 47.
Howard, Elizabeth, wife of Lord Knollys, 24.
Howard, Frances, Countess of Essex, later Countess of Somerset, 24, 26.
Howard, Henry, *see* Earl of Northampton.
Howard, Henry, 32, 38.
Howard, Thomas (1561–1626), *see* Earl of Suffolk.
Howard, Thomas (1586–1646), *see* Earl of Arundel.
Howard, Sir Thomas, 32, 38.
Howard, Thomas, 51.
Howard de Walden, Theophilus, Lord, 63, 118, 120.
Howard of Effingham, William, Lord, 47, 63, 120.
Howard family, 24, 26, 64, 65, 74, 75, 108, 110, 157.
Hunsdon, Lord (John Carey), 32, 38.
Huntingdon, 46.
Huntingdon, Earl of (Henry Hastings), 43–44.
Huntingdonshire, 32.
Hyde, Nicholas, 138, 147.
Hythe, 46.

Impositions: legality of, 8, 94, 99, 120; Neville's suggestions for, 16, 17; Bacon's suggestions for, 21–22, 72; King defends, 99; Commons attack, 8, 91, 94–95, 100–1, 110–12, 114–15, 137–9, 142, 144; Lords debate conference on, 116–22.
Ingram, Sir Arthur, 47.
Ireland, 19, 26, 29, 69, 88, 92, 156.

James I: character and policies, 4–7, 60–61; and Parliament of 1604, 7–9; approached by Neville, 12–13, 16; approached by Bacon, 18; acts as his own secretary, 24; and peerage, 62–63; 1st speech to

Addled Parliament, 80–83; 2nd speech, 88–89; 3rd speech, 99–100; and Neile's case, 129; and dissolution, 136, 139–41; imprisons opposition figures, 146–8; rewards supporters, 148–9; summons parliament again, 155; effects of Addled Parliament on his policies, 157–8; weaknesses of his policy towards parliament, 165–9.
James, Thomas, 39.
James, William, Bishop of Durham, 37, 122.
Jegon, John, Bishop of Norwich, 63.
Jermyn, Sir Thomas, 32.
Johnson, Sir Robert, 46.

Kent, 31, 49, 53.
Kent, William, 49.
Killigrew, Sir Robert, 51, 53, 105.
King's Lynn, 51.
Knaresborough, 46.
Knollys, Sir Robert, 49.
Knollys, Robert, 49.
Knollys, William, Lord, 25, 49, 64, 118, 121, 128, 131, 154, 165.

Lake, Sir Thomas: candidate for secretary of state, 23–24, 74; election to Addled Parliament, 31; appointed to privy council, 74; and supply, 101, 137, 138; attacks established church, 109–10; reports to Commons from King, 135; appointed joint secretary of state, 154–5; mentioned, 75, 79, 84, 94, 102, 165.
Lancashire, 32, 45.
Lancaster, 45.
Laud, William, 116.
Launceston, 48.
Leech, Edward, 48.
Leeds, Sir John, 47.
Leicester, 34, 43–44.
Leigh, Sir Francis, 44.
Lennard, Henry, *see* Lord Dacre.
Lennard, Sampson, 38.
Lennox, Duke of (Ludovic Stuart, Earl of Richmond), 25, 50, 62, 63, 119, 154.

L'Estrange, Sir Hamon, 34–35.
Lincoln, Earl of (Henry Clinton, otherwise Fiennes), 63.
Lincolnshire, 34, 38, 52–53.
Liskeard, 48.
Lisle, Viscount (Robert Sidney), 49, 63, 119–20, 128.
Liverpool, 45.
London, 41–42, 69, 91, 95, 151–2.
Long Parliament, 55–58.
Lorkin, Thomas, 103, 111, 112, 146, 153.
Lostwithiel, 48.
Lovett, Francis, 135–6.
Lowe, Sir Thomas, 41–42.

Manners, Francis, see Earl of Rutland.
Manners, Sir George, 34, 38.
Mansell, Sir Robert, 31, 32, 42, 142.
Manwood, Sir Peter, 31.
Marsham, Germain, 41.
Mary I, 3, 62.
Matthew, Tobias, Archbishop of York, 46, 65, 119.
Middlesex, 31.
Middleton, Sir Hugh, 42.
Middleton, Robert, 42, 91, 101.
Middleton, Sir Thomas, 42.
Monmouth, 46.
Monopolies, 17, 90–91, 95.
Monson, Sir Thomas, 34, 53.
Montague, Sir Henry, 41–42, 59, 93, 94, 102, 111, 141.
Montague, James, Bishop of Bath and Wells, 33, 118, 122.
Montgomery, Earl of (Philip Herbert), 51, 63, 119.
Montgomeryshire, 39.
Moore, Francis, 49, 86, 148.
Moore, Sir Reynolde, 105.
More, Sir George, 32, 59, 85, 93, 94, 95, 100, 102, 126, 127, 137.
More, John, 11.
More, Sir Robert, 105.
Morgan, Thomas, 49.
Mosley, Edward, 45, 102.

Naunton, Robert, 48.
Needham, Robert, 46.
Neile, Richard, Bishop of Lincoln, 116–17, 118, 119, 121, 122, 123–32, 134, 150.
Neville, Christopher, 137, 146–7, 167.
Neville, Edward, see Lord Bergavenny.
Neville, Sir Henry: career, 11; proposals for managing parliament, 11–17, 22, 28, 67–69, 88, 89–90, 112; and undertakers, 12, 106–7, 108–9; candidate for secretary of state, 23, 74; elected to Addled Parliament, 31; mentioned, 59, 75, 137.
Newcastle-under-Lyme, 46.
Newport (Cornwall), 48.
Newton (Lancashire), 46.
Norfolk, 34, 41, 43.
North, Dudley, Lord, 121.
Northampton, 50.
Northampton, Earl of (Henry Howard): leader of Spanish faction, 24–25, 64; opposed a parliament, 26; favours a parliament, 28; and elections, 30, 39, 40, 46–47, 51, 98, 108, 111; promoted to peerage by James, 63; and dissolution, 140, 145; death, 145, 150; mentioned, 29, 68.
Northumberland, 32, 37–38.
Norton, Sir Richard, 35–36.
Norwich, 34.
Nottingham, Earl of (Charles Howard), 32, 47, 63, 80, 108, 118, 121, 128, 131, 154.
Nottinghamshire, 33, 37.

Old Sarum, 48, 49.
Overbury, Sir Thomas, 11, 12, 105, 154, 156.
Owen, Sir Roger: elected to Addled Parliament, 37; and Bacon's eligibility, 85, 87; and undertakers, 97–98, 104–6; attacks impositions, 115; attacks Neile, 124–6, 130–1, 134; mentioned, 60, 146–7, 159.
Oxford, 49.
Oxford University, 39, 57, 58.
Oxfordshire, 31, 37.

Paget, William, Lord, 63.
Parliament, Tudor, 1, 3, 55–58, 159.

INDEX

Parry, Richard, Bishop of St. Asaph, 122.

Parry, Sir Thomas: and financial problem, 10; elected to Addled Parliament, 31; and elections, 43–46; and Stockbridge election, 31, 35, 102–4; expelled from Commons, 56, 103, 107, 162; mentioned, 79, 94, 154, 165, 166.

Paulet, William, see Marquess of Winchester.

Pembroke, Earl of (William Herbert), 25, 28, 39, 47, 48–49, 64, 65, 68, 74, 106, 109, 118, 119, 122, 154.

Penruddock, Sir Thomas, 32.

Penryn, 48.

Perrot, Sir James, 103, 125, 137, 146.

Peterborough, 46.

Petre, William, Lord, 63.

Phelips, Sir Edward, 33, 50, 148.

Phelips, Sir Robert, 13, 33, 48, 52, 102, 123, 125, 126, 148, 160.

Plymouth, 90.

Poole, 49.

Poole, Sir Henry, 98.

Portsmouth, 47.

Poulett, John, 33–34.

Prerogative, 72, 81, 112, 120–2, 131.

Preston, 45.

Price, William, 48.

Principal secretary of state, 23–24, 73–74, 78.

Privileges, 7, 84, 103, 127–8, 164–5.

Privy Council, 25, 26, 27–29, 30, 48, 49, 67–68, 108, 123.

Privy Councillors, 8, 24, 31, 49, 53, 56, 64–65, 66, 104, 128, 150.

Proclamations, 82.

Puritanism: James's attitude towards, 5, 7; and elections to Addled Parliament, 31, 32, 35; strength in Addled Parliament, 57, 60, 94, 95, 136 n.; Winwood and, 76, 110; Neile and, 126; mentioned, 79, 91.

Puysieux, French Envoy, 111–12, 114.

Raleigh, Gilbert, 49.

Raleigh, Sir Walter, 49, 156, 157.

Ravenscroft, William, 49.

Reading, 49.

Reigate, 47.

Reynolds, William, 49.

Rich, Sir Henry, 34–35, 41, 43–44.

Rich, Nathaniel, 51.

Rich, Robert, Lord, 38, 43, 121, 128.

Rich, Sir Robert, 31, 38.

Richmond, Earl of, see Duke of Lennox.

Ripon, 46.

Rivers, Sir George, 46.

Robinson, Henry, Bishop of Carlisle, 63.

Rochester, 30, 42–43, 53.

Rochester, Viscount, see Earl of Rochester.

Roe, Sir Thomas, 115, 125, 134, 137.

Roman Catholicism, 6, 25, 31, 64, 75, 79, 81, 88, 91, 92, 98, 130.

Romney, 47.

Rowlands, Henry, Bishop of Bangor, 63.

Rudd, Anthony, Bishop of St. David's, 63.

Russell, Francis, Lord, 63.

Rutland, Earl of (Francis Manners), 33, 34, 38, 52.

Rye, 47.

Sackville, Richard, see Earl of Dorset.

St. Albans, 50.

St. Ives, 48.

St. John, Oliver, Lord, 118.

St. John, —, 45.

St. Mawes, 48.

Salisbury, 1st Earl of (Robert Cecil), Lord Treasurer and Secretary, 8, 12, 16, 19, 23, 25, 51, 76.

Salisbury, 2nd Earl of (William Cecil), 48–49, 150.

Saltash, 33, 42, 48.

Sammes, Sir John, 105.

Sandwich, 47.

Sandys, Sir Edwin: opposition leader, 19; defeated in election to Addled Parliament in Kent, 31, 49, 53; elected to Addled Parliament, 42–43, 53; opposes imposi-

Sandys, Sir Edwin (*cont.*)
tions, 100, 101, 110, 111, 115, 142; and Parry's case, 103; and Neile's case, 125, 130; linked with Howards, 108; mentioned, 37, 59, 132, 144, 146, 159.

Sandys, Sir Miles, 39–41.

Sandys, Sir Samuel, 37, 127.

Sarmiento, Don Diego, Spanish Ambassador, 65, 79, 139–40, 154, 156–7.

Savile, Sir John, 60, 85, 146.

Saye and Sele, Lord, 131.

Scotland, 4, 5, 156.

Scudamore, Sir James, 32.

Selby, Sir George, 37–38.

Selby, Ralph, 37.

Selby, Sir William, 32, 38.

Seymour, Edward, *see* Earl of Hertford.

Shaftesbury, 48.

Sharpe, Lionel, 140, 146.

Sheffield, Edmund, Lord, 74.

Shirley, Sir Thomas, 48.

Short Parliament, 55.

Shropshire, 37.

Sidney, Robert, *see* Viscount Lisle.

Sidney, Sir Robert, 49.

Smith, Sir Nicholas, 48.

Smyth, Sir Thomas, 47.

Somerset, 33, 52, 91.

Somerset, Earl of (Robert Carr, previously Viscount Rochester): supports Neville for secretary of state, 11, 12, 16; marries Frances Howard, 24; supports Spanish faction, 25, 26, 64, 65; and elections, 30, 42; raised to peerage by James I, 63; supports Winwood for secretary, 74, 75; contributes to benevolence, 150; opposes a parliament, 153; mentioned, 27, 28, 29, 35, 68, 79, 119, 140.

Somerset, Edward, *see* Earl of Worcester.

Somerset, Henry, *see* Lord Herbert.

Southampton, Earl of (Henry Wriothesley), 11, 62–63, 65, 74, 117, 119, 121, 131, 143.

Spain, 6, 75, 114–15, 124, 139, 154, 155, 156–7, 158.

Spanish Faction, 25, 64, 65, 73, 108–9, 140, 153, 154.

Speaker, 21, 41–42, 83–84, 85–86, 93, 126–7, 129, 138–9, 141, 148.

Spelman, Sir Henry, 51.

Spencer, Robert, Lord, 119, 121, 131.

Spiller, Henry, 109.

Stanhope, John, Lord, 165.

Stockbridge, 31, 35, 45, 102–3.

Strode, Sir William, 123, 138.

Stuart, Ludovic, *see* Duke of Lennox.

Suckling, John, 47.

Sudbury, 46.

Suffolk, 32.

Suffolk, Earl of (Thomas Howard): and elections to Addled Parliament, 32, 34, 38, 48; and undertakers, 68, 108; and impositions, 118, 122; defends Neile, 129, 131; and dissolution, 143; contributes to benevolence, 150; lord treasurer, 152–3; mentioned, 63, 154.

Supply: Neville's plans for, 15, 17, 67; Bacon's plans for, 19, 71–73; King requests from Addled Parliament, 81, 88–89, 99–100; Officials request from Addled Parliament, 91–93; Commons postpones, 93, 95, 97, 100, 101, 111–12; Commons refuses to vote, 136–9, 141–2, 144–5.

Surrey, 32.

Sussex, 39.

Swaffham, 34.

Taunton, 50.

Thetford, 46.

Thomas, Mr., 52.

Thornborough, John, Bishop of Bristol, 135.

Tichbourne, Sir Richard, 35–37.

Totnes, 30, 51.

Toursom, Mr., 41.

Towse, William, 148.

Tracy, Sir Thomas, 51.

Tregony, 48.

Trevor, Sir John, 47.

Truro, 48.

Tuchet, George, *see* Lord Audley.

Tudor Dynasty, 1, 2, 3, 169.

INDEX

Undertakers: Neville's plans and, 12, 15, 68–69, 106; Bacon and, 70–71, 73, 98–99; King and, 81, 88–89, 100; Commons and, 93, 94, 95, 97–98, 104–6; Stockbridge case, 102–3; effects of, 106–9, 163.
Uvedale, Sir William, 35–37.

Vane, Sir Henry, 48.
Vavasor, Sir Thomas, 47.
Venetian Ambassador, 10, 106, 154.
Venice, 23, 114.
Vivian, Francis, 48.

Waad, Sir William, 23.
Wales, 90.
Wallingford, 49.
Wallop, Sir Henry, 35–37, 45, 53.
Walsingham, Sir Thomas, 31.
Walsingham, Sir Thomas, Jr., 49.
Walter, Sir William, 144.
Wars of the Roses, 2.
Watson, Thomas, 47, 135.
Wentworth, Peter, 50.
Wentworth, Thomas, son of Peter Wentworth, 91, 115–16, 123, 137, 146–7.
Wentworth, Sir Thomas, later Earl of Strafford, 160.
West, Thomas, see Lord de la Warr.
West Looe, 48.
Westmorland, 38.
Weston, Sir Richard, 31.
Wharton, Philip, Lord, 38.
Wharton, Sir Thomas, 38.
Whitelocke, James, 50–51, 53, 87, 93, 94–95, 100, 160.
Whitson, John, 138.
Widdrington, Sir Henry, 37.
Wigan, 46.
Wilbraham, Sir Roger, 32.
Williamson, Sir Richard, 87.

Willoughby de Eresby, Lord (Robert Bertie), 34, 38.
Wilton, 49.
Wiltshire, 32, 38, 49.
Winchelsea, 47.
Winchester, 36.
Winchester, Marquess of (William Paulet), 62.
Winwood, Sir Ralph: candidate for secretary of state, 23; appointed, 74; never in Commons before 1614, 58; career and character, 75–77; maiden speech, 83; and Bacon's eligibility, 86–87; and supply, 91–94, 101, 112, 138, 142, 144–5; problems, 96, 165–7; and Parry's case, 102–3; attacks established church, 109–10; defends impositions, 114–15; and Neile's case, 124, 127; and dissolution, 141, 142; and benevolence, 150–1; mentioned, 11, 79, 84, 111, 154.
Wolverston, Robert, 148.
Woodstock, 51.
Worcester, Earl of (Edward Somerset), 25, 63, 118, 128.
Worcestershire, 37.
Wotton, Edward, Lord, 23, 25, 154, 165.
Wotton, Sir Henry, 23–24, 59, 73–74, 114, 115, 142.
Wriothesley, Henry, see Earl of Southampton.
Wymarke, Edward, 45, 46.
Wynn, Richard, 32.

Yelverton, Sir Henry, 50, 59, 90, 111.
Yorkshire, 46.

Zouch, Lord (Edward la Zouch), 25, 118, 122, 129, 154.

Date Due

PRINTED IN U. S. A.